An Oregon Tale

(The memoirs of one man's failed attempt to escape childhood)

By
Dave Whiteman
"To error is human, to write about it takes a really twisted mind"

ISBN: 1-58500-155-4

These are the tales of Dave's adventurous, yet accident filled, youth set in a mostly rural environment. These stories will make you laugh until you cry, scratch your head in total puzzlement, just plain cry and then laugh some more, all the while bringing back many memories of your own childhood, or thankful that these weren't your childhood memories. Some of his laughter and pain, may be your own gain.

His body of work has been compared to a cross between Patrick McManus and Garrison Keillor. His body has been compared to a cross between Fabio and Woody Allen. His mind has been compared to a cross between Shakespeare and biscuits & gravy.

His stories are a down home account of the last forty years in this changing world. Most are of his youth but some also blend the past with the present. These tales take the reader back to simpler times of days gone by in a wonderful state called Oregon. The stories are all true and as he says, "There are plenty of court records, witnesses, physical and emotional scars to prove all of them!"

The book contains 65 chapters and these are but a few of the many subjects and exploits within:

How Nutria came to Oregon - Little Connestogas or Spaceships?
What mice and the Boot Scoot Boogie have in common,
What the police did with the dead deer riding Dave's bicycle,
Skinny-dipping with monsters,
What love and moonstruck watermelon have in common,
Elvis and the bloated cow,

Raiding apple orchards at midnight,
Why streaking and strolling are not conducive,
Crawling naked into a nutria den,
Why sometimes FIRE! Just happens,
What NOT to do when FIRE! Just happens,
Fighting Dust Spitting Cobras on a Christmas Tree farm,
What 007, Calvin Klein, J.Edgar Hoover, and the Beatles
had to do with bean picking,
Hitchhiking do's and don'ts,
The dangers of troutsicles,
Why cats, pistachio's and bicycles can't be trusted,
The downside to converting a chicken coop into a sauna,
(Believe it or not, there is also an upside)
Surviving your siblings in the country,
Seeking fame and fortune in Alaska,
Porcupines in my pants,
And many, many more.

MY SUMMER VACATION

In the summer of 88, I loaded my family into our antique VW Camper bus with enough food and gear to outfit an expedition. We were heading for a high mountain lake for a week of camping and fishing. We were pumped, we were excited, but alas, we were doomed. For starters we were heading out in the middle of the day in the middle of a heat wave. Fortunately we had three bored, restless, screaming boys, plus a half of a ton of camping gear and food to transport to the top of a high mountain pass in a twenty year old, under powered, over loaded, air-cooled VW, with a loose fan belt and an oil leak. My philosophy of "Ignore it and it will go away" was about to be put to the test.

We were quite away up the pass and maintaining a cruising speed of anywhere between 17 and 23 mph. Behind us was a line of cars stretching for about three miles. They must have sensed our Brady Bunch happiness because they were all waving at us, and of course my kids were waving back. I can only assume they were waving out of a similar sense of happiness and camaraderie to be on the road together, in spite of such a numerous amount of clenched fists.

We soon passed a sign on our right announcing a scenic viewpoint up ahead. Now given the fact that we were driving so slowly, we had ample time to decide whether or not to pull out of our own personal line of traffic and enjoy the view. But like all married couples, much discussion comes up first.

" *Do you want to pull over?* "

" *I don't care, what do you want to do?* "

" *It doesn't matter to me*".

And so, before this discussion is finished (and believe me, they never are) we have missed our scenic viewpoint pullout, and continue on our way.

We are but ten minutes from the summit, and no more then twenty minutes from the cool, clear mountain lake of our destination. I can smell the pine trees, I can smell the campfire with fresh caught trout cooking over it, I can also smell red hot metal and motor oil with no more viscosity!

We are less than a mile from the top of the mountain and my cruising speed is 12 mph and dropping rapidly. My wife asks why the engine sounds so funny at 7 mph. Over the horrible noise the engine is making, I politely yell " *Shut up dear, I have to think*". I am now having trouble thinking at 4 mph, in first gear, at full throttle. I pulled over into the red lava dust on the side of the road. I didn't have to turn off the engine, it managed this on it's own. I got out of the bus to take a look at the engine. I have to say it certainly looked OK, it just smelled something awful.

I needed to think. I needed a cigarette. I lit one off the glowing red-hot engine, giving me my first clue as to the depth of our trouble. I glanced at the now rapidly moving line of air conditioned, water-cooled cars driving past, still waving, although smiling now. My kids continued waving back.

I climbed back into the bus and looked at that woman I had married so long ago. Because of the heat, she was wringing wet and had kind of a surly look. Her sunglasses seemed to be melting as they slid off her nose. I chose not to mention it. I did mention however that our engine had died a cruel death, and we would probably die as well before help could be summoned. She looked at me and I could see fear in her eyes. I looked in the mirror and could see fear in my eyes. I looked at the sweaty creatures in the back of the bus, and I could see **Evil** in their eyes! I calmly said " ***DON'T ANYBODY PANIC!*** " but I could see it was too late. We were on the verge of a full-scale riot.

My wife gave each one of the child creatures some sort of chocolate stuff and sent them out into the red lava dust to play. Not a smart thing to do at 103 degrees, but again I chose not to mention it. I decided our best chance for rescue was for me to dust off my thumb and hitchhike into the next town for help.

No one seemed interested in giving me a ride however, and I suspected it had to do with the chocolate and red lava dust covered child-like creatures lurking in the shade of the roadside bushes. They even gave me the shivers!

After about ten minutes of unsuccessful hitchhiking, Chris, my two-year-old, broke from the pack and wandered my way pushing his toy lawnmower in front of him. He stops, and looks up adoringly at his daddy. He is barefoot, wearing only a drooping diaper, and is covered in chocolate and sweat. His tearstained cheeks, and the rest of his half sweat/half chocolate body is highlighted with red lava dust. I smile, and put him in front of me, with one hand on his head, the other in full hitchhiking mode and off we walk down the highway, mower and all. The third car that passed this spectacle did a quick double take and pulled over.

The nice old man at the wheel, mentioned that he never picks up hitchhikers, but it seemed to him that we had with us, what appeared to be children. He kindly towed us into the next town where the only mechanic on the mountain, pronounced our engine DOA.

At this point I called my friend Bob, who also had a <u>Classic</u> VW Camper-bus. Now in order to call your vehicle a classic, it has to meet the following criteria:

1) It has to be old

2) It must never run extremely well

3) You have to sink more money into it than you can ever hope to get out of it.

On retrospect most all of my prior vehicles would be considered <u>Classics</u>. Anyway, I conveyed my situation and dilemma to Bob, who upon finding out where we were, immediately said, *"You went right pass the scenic viewpoint didn't you*?" He then explained that we should have pulled over and let our engine cool off with all the other VW's trying to climb the mountain that day. Apparently the mountain pass we tried to conquer, fully loaded, mid day, during a heat wave, was long ago dubbed by experienced VW enthusiasts, as <u>*Bus-Eater Pass.*</u>

We called a tow truck. The driver looked us over fairly well, which I'm sure aided his decision to allow us to ride in our own bus, thereby protecting the cab of his truck from such a motley crew as we. So we all piled into the camper, and off we rode off into the sunset, on rear wheels alone, eating cold fried chicken and potato salad, while staring at the back of the tow truck driver's head.

JUST RAMBLIN

Like most people, I came into this world barefoot. Growing up in the country, I remained that way most of the time. The hazards were rusty nails, stickers, slivers, slugs and that other "S" word, doodoo. Some doodoo's are more feared than others. Chicken and dog doodoo topping the list. Organic Frisbees (cow doodoo) frequently flip you so that you find yourself sitting in it. Road Apples (horse doodoo) pose no threat as you can juggle 'em, throw 'em, even play golf or baseball with 'em- although you can't hit 'em very far.

The best part of being barefoot in the country is of course, some nice thick, creamy mud oozing up through your toes, causing hours of entertainment. A country road with four inches of flour like dust is the most tranquil for your feet. You hear and feel a "poof" with each step, and little clouds of dust follow you- which every child knows, confuses the beasts that are stalking you.

A long time ago I was traveling by thumb and found myself in West Palm Beach, Florida. It was 8:00 A.M., I had just changed my clothes in a culvert, and had scrambled up on the highway. I was wondering what lay in store for me on this hot humid day in a faraway land, when a low flying bird said good morning, and doodooed on my shoulder. Sadly enough, that was the high point of that day.

Two decades later, while taking out the garbage, another low flying bird said good morning on my shoulder. The mystic in me asked "*Is this a sign, and what does it mean?*" The realist in me merely said what the bird had done. My children however, seemed to think it suitable punishment for a man forever yelling at them to put their shoes on when they play outside.

The Turbulent Sixties

It was a time of uncertainty, rioting, and social unrest. And this was just at my house. My older brothers liked to play this game called Slugabug. The rules were simple enough. Whenever we rode in the car and one of them would spot a V.W. Beetle,

(now what were the odds of that happening in the sixties), they would yell "*Slugabug*" and then slug my kid brother and I. Call it a great game if you like, personally, I hated car trips.

One time they thought it would be cute to stuff my kid brother and I into separate gunnysacks and sew them shut. They then drug us over to the edge of the highway. For added effect they told us to peer through the gunnysack so that we could see the white paint of the highway. At this point they convinced us that this was the center line and that if we rolled in any direction we would be run over by the many trucks that went by our place en-route to the mill, or on into town. So here are my two older brothers, standing on the edge of the highway with two gunny-sacks full of siblings and to make matters worse, they were pulling their arms up and down causing the big rigs to blow their horns. To this day I can still hear the air horns and worse yet the compression brakes the trucks would use to slow down to make the turn to the mill. The highway would vibrate and my kid brother and I would just tremble. When my folks got home that night I told them "*Your not gonna believe what Jim and Doug did to us this time, **Now kill them**!*"

My folks refused to kill them. Needless to say my older brothers were a frisky bunch.

Another time, my kid brother was chasing me with a

fishing pole, swearing he was going to hook me with it. As I felt the hook sink in, I yelled "*DON'T SET THE HOOK, YOU GOT ME*!" He had hooked me in the eyelid. We somehow made it into the house, where I immediately said to my mom " *Look what Dan did, **Now kill him**!*"

She refused to kill him. Dan became an avid fisherman and I like to think I had something to do with it.

During another skirmish, Dan was chasing me with an ax, hell bent on my demise. For your information, a hatchet is the length of a small boy's arm. An ax is as long as the small boy carrying it, and appears approximately twice as long as the small boy running from it. Finding no place to hide, I jumped up on an old post and tried to reason with him. I knew diplomacy had failed by the look in his eye and the grin on his face. He swung that big ax with all he had, and the blade went smack between my big toe and the one next to it.

Aside from ruining my rubber boots, no harm was done. I ran into the house and told my mom "*Look what Dan did, **Now kill him**!*" Again, she refused, even though blatant disregard for rubber boots was considered a felony at our house.

I retaliated a few years later. I had gotten home from school one day and spotted him in the backyard, bent over, looking for something in the grass. He didn't know I was home yet, much less in the house. My course was clear. I loaded my dad's deer rifle and crept into the bathroom. Ever so quietly, I slid open the window. While he was bent over, in deep concentration, I squeezed the trigger and blew a hole out of the ground, right under his nose. As I was running for my life, I couldn't help but chuckle over how I had finally bested him. The chuckling of course stopped, when he finally caught me.

While writing this article, the bloodcurdling screams coming from my boy's room make me wonder if the nineties won't be a little turbulent also.

BARPITS

"*Hey, where's the dog, has anybody seen the dog today*?" I would ask. "*Check the barpits*" My mom would answer. "*Check the barpits*". What a strange sounding word. My folks, you see, called ditches, barpits. I've always been grateful that they hadn't named me Ditches Barpits. Although when I consider the amount of time I spent in them, it probably would've been appropriate.

When I was about eight, we were at a friend's place up Woods Creek Road, at the base of Mary's Peak. I found myself sailing down a hill, at light speed, on a bike which I then discovered had no brakes. I had three choices. Dead ahead (and I do mean **dead ahead**) was a fifteen foot drop off into Woods Creek, to my left was a barpit, and to my right was the trusty family VW bus. I think it was the warm smile on the front of the bus that made me choose it to stop my flight.

When I came to, my mom wrapped my broken arm in an Avon catalog and drove me to the hospital. I had broken my other arm when I was four, and hadn't liked it, so all the way to the hospital I kept asking if my arm was broken. My mom kept telling me that it was only a compound fracture. At the hospital a nurse met us at the door, looked at my arm and shouted, "*GOOD LORD, this boy has a compound fracture*!" My mom, still trying to comfort me, said "*Yes, we know, but at least it's not broken.*"

When I was ten, I got on a brand new, borrowed ten speed. I didn't know about hand brakes, and as it had no foot brakes, where my frantic backpedaling didn't stop me, a four-foot barpit did.

When I was twelve, I was riding my bike down a gravel

road with a field burn going on both sides. I often crossed that fine line between bravery and stupidity. When the smoke got too thick too see, I got off and walked my bike in the darkness. I was barefoot, and had felt my way down about a hundred feet of the road, when suddenly, without warning, the left barpit reached up and drug myself and my sorry little bike into it's depths. I felt the left side of my left foot go completely numb. I drug myself and my bike back up onto the road, and continued my journey. After a couple a hundred more feet I made it out of the smoke, to discover that I had slashed my foot to the bone. My mom once again drove me to the hospital. Oddly enough I have no ill feelings towards barpits. Bicycles on the other hand, can seldom be trusted.

WITH A SONG IN MY HEART

It was one of those hot humid days of August, and I was zipping along a country road in a shiny red convertible. Okay, so it was a dusty, red Massey Ferguson windrower and my zipping only amounted to about 13 M.P.H., but it <u>was</u> a really hot day. I was seventeen, clad only in tenny-runners and a pair of boxer shorts, with little hearts and tigers on them. I was driving, standing up, wind in my face, singing" *BORN FREE!!!"* Yes, the world was my oyster. Suddenly, a horn honked and a friend of mine, with a girl in a bikini, shot past me in a real convertible. The oyster was now gone, and I found myself singing *"ONLY THE LONELY, dumdumdumdumdididoowahh!!!"*

A few years later I was making my daily commute to the sawmill on that very same road. It was winter, I was riding a little tiny motorcycle, and wearing a set of canary yellow rain gear. My chin was resting on the handlebars (you had to do that to break the 42m.p.h. barrier) and I was singing the theme song from Superchicken, " *WHEN YOU FIND YOURSELF IN DANGER, WHEN YOUR THREATENED BY A STRANGER, WHEN IT LOOKS LIKE YOU WILL TAKE A LICKIN, BOCKBOCKBOCKBOCK, CALL ON SUPERCHICKEN"*

During my hitchhiking days I sang *"COUNTRY ROADS"* so much that I was starting to detest John Denver. While on a Caribbean cruise I was stuck on that Foster Farm jingle *"OH THAT FARM FRESH CHICKEN"* My wife was starting to detest me. Sometimes I'd make up songs like *"YOU CALLED MY NAME, I START TO CRY, I STUCK MY FORK, RIGHT IN MY EYE"* Or the ever popular *"WHO CAN COOK SOME PORK HEARTS, MIX IN TONGUES AND FEET, PULL OUT ALL THE BONES*

AND MAKE A TASTY BREAKFAST TREAT, THE SCRAPPLE MAN CAN"

When I listen to the radio I hum, if there is no radio I sing, So don't be alarmed if you catch me in the meat-cooler, far from the reach of the Safeway Radio Network, perched on a pallet of chickens belting out *"ooooooooooooooOKLAHOMA!!!"*

JUST BECAUSE I'M NOT PARANOID, DOESN'T MEAN THAT THEY'RE NOT OUT TO GET ME

When I was a kid we had chores. They varied with the seasons. There was wood to be stacked, hay to be hauled, dishes done, laundry folded, horse stalls to be shoveled, etc. For your information, a small boy <u>cannot</u> out shovel three horses. Most chores if forgotten, could be done the following day, some could not.

My dad would ask me if I had fed the horses. I had forgotten to do it after school (when the sun was up) and now had to do it after supper (when the sun was down!)

There were no lights in the barn, and fear would make me walk to it so slowly that I could hear my hair grow. A flake of straw and a coffee can of grain later my task was done, **but,** I still had to survive the trip back to the house. No monsters in sight, but nonetheless there, I would try to walk bravely back to the house. The closer I got, the faster I'd run- until I'd finally burst through the door, slam it, lock it, and then lean against it, trying to catch my breath.

At that point a family member would usually make a comment about how **IT** almost got me that time. On occasion, if they were in one of their cruel moods, they would turn out the light and lock the back door while I was in mid-flight. I grew up in a close knit, but slightly twisted family.

Sometimes I would lie in bed and dangle one foot over the edge. I would then suddenly remember about the monster under the bed that was about to bite my foot off. Deep down I knew that only old socks and lint were under my bed. But deeper down I knew that old socks and lint are two of the three things that monsters feed on, the third being small feet. So what do I do with my poor little foot? Leave it dangle and be a mature, fearless, one-legged child? I think not.

Unfortunately this sort of paranoia passes from father to son. When my son Jesse was five, I took him to an Oregon State University basketball game. Before the game started, the ROTC squad came marching onto the floor. Half were carrying flags, the other half were shouldering rifles. Jesse looked at me, and said, "*I know dad, whoever wins the game gets the flags, and whoever loses gets shot!*" I patted him on the head and said " *That's right son.*"

TAKE TWO ASPIRIN

I suffer from a rare disorder known as Repetitive Stupitosis. I can remember once in junior high school, holding a pencil in my hand while resting my top teeth on the erasure. (Why, is not important here) The pencil slipped, skidded over my lip, missed my nose (Thank God!) and landed in my eye. It wasn't until the third assault on my eye that I finally put my pencil away.

On another occasion I decided to try shaving with an old-fashioned six-inch straight razor. I lathered up my little face and immediately made a two-inch slice down my cheek. Blood doesn't get any redder than when it is on a background of shaving cream. A few weeks later, with a healed face, I tried it again. On the same cheek, on the same spot, I made the same two-inch slice.

Another malady of mine is Lazy Feet. My parents say I use to trip over the white line on a gymnastics mat. Many fellow employees have witnessed my tripping over <u>nothing</u>, on the sales floor. I jokingly refer to this as "Instant Traction", but it is indeed "Lazy Feet". One time while deer hunting, I was climbing into my dad's truck, tripped, and shot a hole through his windshield. I told my dad that it was the sickness and offered my entire bean picking money to fix it. Even though that money was earmarked for a Sears-Roebuck couch that folded into a pool table.

Lackacaffeinitis struck a few winters back when I went up on the roof to clean the chimney. At the crack of dawn I climbed out of my upstairs window, and unknowingly onto an ice patch. I started sliding down the roof. Knowing what lay ahead, I assumed the downhill skiing crouch. When I came to the edge of the roof I jumped not unlike the ski jumpers on *Wide World of Sports*. Lackacaffeinitis kept my cat-like reflexes from working properly, and I landed much like the *Agony of Defeat* section of that same program.

For safety's sake I now try to ingest at least one cup of coffee before leaving my bed each day.

TINY BUBBLES

Quite possibly the only thing more exhilarating than a roomful of women exchanging labor stories, is a roomful of men swapping hernia tales. This tale is mine.

I remember lying in my hospital bed worrying about my upcoming operation. I was in the hospital because I had failed the much dreaded " Turn your head and cough" test a few days earlier. I was lying there, as men do, wondering why my life had been cut short at age 26, when suddenly a male nurse poked his head into the room and sneered " *Here's Johnny*! " Before I could ask this clown what he wanted, he flings back my covers, whips out a razor, and say's he is here to shave me! Before I could scream and/or run away, he had taken hold of the situation- if you know what I mean, and I think you do.

His job now complete, I lay there thinking about the indignity of it all, and how this man was most definitely underpaid, when two thug like interns burst into my room, throw me on a gurney, wheel me down a hall and into an operating room, knock me out, cut two holes in me, theoretically fix something, sew me back up, wheel me back into my room and throw me onto the bed in an unconscious heap.

I was groggy when I awoke not fully knowing whom, or where I was. My subconscious however, knew exactly what was going on and without my permission, reached over, grabbed, and lit a cigarette. Not knowing how or why I was holding this burning stick, I scan the room for anything resembling an ashtray. My eyes semi-focus on a Styrofoam tray. My thinking was to spit into the tray and put out this burning stick. I don't know if any of you has ever tried to spit after major surgery, but when I tried all that came out was a pitiful little herd of tiny bubbles. I then proceeded to stick the cigarette <u>through</u> the Styrofoam tray, knocking the red hot cherry onto my gown. Still groggy, but now sort of on fire, I weakly brush the coals off of my gown and onto my bed. Starting to panic just a little now, I blow some more bubbles at the embers and manage to brush them onto the floor.

I fall exhausted back into bed wondering if my medical insurance has a fire clause, when a Nurse Ratchet storms into my room, tries to get me to voluntarily get out of bed, and say's "*You must go to the bathroom*!" Through slurred speech, tiny bubbles and sign language, I try to explain to her that if I sit up my stomach will rip open, and an alien will jump out wreaking much havoc upon her and the hospital. Ignoring my warning, She grabbed me like a ragdoll, pulled me out of bed, and once again said, " *You must go to the bathroom*!" I looked at the floor and gasped "*You mean (bubble) right here (bubble) right now*?!" She looked me over as if in search of fresh lobotomy scars, and having found none, pointed rather sternly towards the lavatory. Still heavily medicated, I tried to explain to her that I couldn't very well walk way over there, as I didn't seem to have my legs with me, and if they didn't show up pretty soon, heads were gonna roll. She sighed, put my arm around her neck, wiped the bubbles off my lips, and muttered something to the effect that since I could talk without a brain, I could surely walk without legs. And I'll be darned if she wasn't right.

A Life of Grime

I guess for me, it all started in 1959 at this great state's centennial celebration. My folks were walking around looking at all the sights with their five kids. I was five years old and apparently hungry because while my mom was holding my left hand, my right hand was frantically trying to grasp a half eaten hot-dog I had spotted on the ground. Long before I had ever heard the word <u>recycling</u> I had grasped it's significance. I had also managed to grasp the hot-dog, but <u>you know who</u> made me throw it back from whence it came.

Whether you are aware of it or not, you all recycle. Those of you who shop at garage sales, flea markets, second hand stores, or just find another use for something otherwise destined for the garbage can, are recycling.

When I was a kid, we used to gravitate towards dumps. Abandoned or active, no matter where we were, we could find them. Whether we were called environmentalists, archeologists, or scavengers- whatever we were called, fell on deaf ears as we were to busy looking for really neat stuff. Today, as a mature (?) adult, I no longer do much dumpster diving. However, if a really choice piece is spotted on the top half of a dumpster, it will probably find it's way into my garage for later use.

A very good friend of mine had a big dumpster behind his auto-body shop in Eugene. He used to cruise through it on a regular basis to find out what all had been illegally thrown into it during the twilight hours. One day he found several boxes of brand new oak bathroom fixtures, towel holders, bathrobe holders, miscellaneous plumbing hardware, etc. He found so many different things that he eventually began to refer to it as his magic dumpster.

Swear to god, one day he was plowing through his magic dumpster to discover that he was standing on the undercarriage of a car. He started kicking stuff off of the car, when he realized that (being an auto-body man) what he was standing on was a stripped down, cut in two, obviously stolen, Porsche. He hauled all the salvageable pieces out, and eventually used them all in his business. Made a pretty penny in the process too.

Recently, on an early morning bike ride, I collected 51 empty beer and pop cans (value-$2.55) and a really neat pair of Italian jogging shoes (street value- $3.00.) All of these were destined for the dump instead of into my wallet and onto my feet.

During the late 80's, I was taking my three boys for a walk through our little town's college campus. I had forgotten to bring a sack to carry empties with, so I had to resort to putting my finger into the hole of each can I would find in order to carry them. Pretty soon I had a can on each finger of each hand, at which point my four year old Chris, started calling me "Edward Beercanhands."

Over the last quarter of a century I have walked more miles, on more stretches of highway, in more states, than I can remember. I am always amazed at the treasures to be found alongside the road and in the ditches. I have acquired a keen eye for what is out of place along the side of the road.

Some of the roadside treasures have been literally hundreds of tools, a full tool box, an empty tool box, a motorcycle helmet, a motorcycle (two separate occasions), and a brand spanking new, still in the box, set of car seat covers, that I desperately needed but couldn't afford.

Now I'll be the first to admit that part of my motives are financial (revenues from empty beer cans are nontaxable) but mostly I just like leaving places cleaner than when I got there, although you might not believe it by looking in my boy's room.

All of us want a cleaner place to live, and we can all make it that way. Whether your walking in a wilderness area, or just walking around the block, if every time you go somewhere you pick up just one piece of litter, you just made the world a cleaner place. And who knows, you just might find a really neat pair of Italian jogging shoes!

Wheels

It seemed like everyone at my high school drove a really nice car. The parking lot was full of sports cars, muscle-cars, convertibles, trucks, and Jeeps. They were all beauties and envied by those of us still saving for our first set of wheels.

I had saved all my money from farming all summer and flipping burgers all winter. Across the street from the burger stand sat a dandy of a Corvette for sale for right at $2000. I was making $1.20 an hour, and tried to figure out how many decades it would take to buy that car. Since these were the days prior to both hand-held calculators, and creative financing, it didn't take too much ciphering on my part to realize I might have to settle for a little less car.

So I saved and I saved, until one spring day found me cruising to school behind the wheel of a shiny white, 1965 Rambler 440 Classic. It had four doors, a three on the tree, and six cylinders of ground-pounding (yet economical) power. All those kids in their fancy cars must've secretly envied mine, since they wouldn't even park near it. One bonus feature was that the whole front seat reclined into the back seat turning my dream machine into a love nest as well. Find me a Corvette that will do that.

Besides a fair amount of moonlit romancing, I used to take the car hunting and four wheeling a lot. Between the posi-trac and the trunk-load of newspapers I kept in it, she was a hill-climbing beast.

There was one hill in particular, that I had only seen Jeeps make to the top. It was a dream of mine to make it up there in my Rambler. It was about five hundred feet of bumps and ruts, with the last half about twice as steep as the first. At this point you would enter a stand of trees where it got real dark, and real ugly. I had been to the edge of the trees before, but never had the traction to finish on through to the top.

One fall day found me giving it yet another shot. Soil conditions were perfect, and the feeling in my gut told me that today's attempt would be like no other. I took a deep breath, punched the gas, and hit the hill doing about 35mph. I flew through the curvy chute, rode the ruts perfectly and crested the first small hill faster than I had ever been before. I then began that long kidney jarring, wheel-spinning climb towards the top.

I knew at this point that after all my failed attempts, I was finally going to enter the trees. But just before I did, through all the bouncing, and without warning, my reclining front seat, did just that. I found myself in a prone position, staring at my dome light. As I was now flat on my back, I began to notice a series of things, such as my hands were no longer on the steering wheel, and my feet were no longer anywhere near the gas, clutch, or most importantly at this point, the brake. The car (now sort of on auto-pilot) slowly stopped bouncing up the hill, and rather quickly started bouncing down the hill backwards, thus proving the what goes up theory.

Now as a high strung high schooler, this was NOT the kind of bouncing I had envisioned when I bought the car. Fortunately I wound up back at the bottom of the hill with little damage to my car or myself. After my nerves had settled, I realized that I had to make a decision between a romancing rig and a four wheeling rig. Having decided that, a few weeks later found me driving to school behind the wheel of a 1962, hand painted, coppertone brown, four wheel drive International Scout. The boys in their fancy-cars still wouldn't park near me, although one guy in a John

Deere did.

Gone Fishin

Recently, thanks to several good friends, I have been reintroduced to the joys of fishing. I have always maintained that you don't go fishing for the fish- and I think you'll see why.

When we were little, our grandpa bought each one of us kids a cane pole and he, our dad, and our uncle Don, showed us some knots, and took us to water. We fished every river, slow river, dead river, slough, ditch, and settling pond in our corner of the valley. One special place in particular was the Mary's River Dam. The dam, if memory serves me, was maybe 60 to 80 feet in length, 15 to 20 feet high, and had about a six-foot wide ledge at the water's edge. Perfect for diving from, or fishing off of, or just sitting there dangling your feet in the water. On the right side of the dam was a fish ladder, and just a little downstream was where we would camp. It was a wonderful spot with tall trees, shallow water, and little current.

Often as not during these trips, aunts, uncles, and other clan members would camp with us. The grown-ups would busy themselves with pitching tents, tethering horses, cooking, smoking, kicking dogs, whooping kids, and occasionally taking a snort of what they referred to as snake bite remedy. I couldn't understand why they would take a snort before they were bitten, I always thought you took it after a bite. Looking back on it now, I realize that it was not only a remedy but must have been a repellent as well. It must've worked because I can't remember any one getting bit, although some of the adults were a little slow out of the gate the next morning.

The dozen or so of us kids would help set up camp by

running, swimming, eating, fighting, cutting our feet on broken glass, and maybe a little more eating. It was a pretty good system. We were all like farts in a skillet, taking off in 360 degrees, each going on their own adventure. Periodically, a concerned adult would bang on a skillet, honk a horn, or if all else failed, my mom would just snap her finger, and all kids would return to camp for a head count. There would always be one or two kids missing, but the adults agreed that 12, out of 13 or 14 kids, was a pretty good percentage and off we'd run again. Until of course, my mom would snap her finger, returning us all back to camp once again. My mom could snap her finger and make a deer bolt at just under three hundred yards.

While the rest of us kids were getting into just the right amount of mischief, brother Doug was busy building a wooden raft. When he was satisfied that it was indeed seaworthy, he fashioned a sandbox in the middle of it. He then loaded it with firewood, and his fishing pole, and pushed it out into the middle of the river just below the dam. The sandbox would contain the fire that he would build on it for that night's catfishing. I can't tell you if he caught any fish, or even if the raft survived the fire, but I can tell you that he was the envy of all of us bare-footers stuck on shore.

The rest of us built fires all along the shore, including one on the ledge of the dam. As night fell, we drug our sleeping bags up and over the fish ladder, down the spillway, and over to the fire, and commenced catfishing. We fished until sleep took us one by one. Come sunrise, there was still a little smoke coming out of the fire, and a half dozen kids sprawled out all over the dam. Not one kid rolled off the dam and into the river that night, but I do think we lost a sleeping bag to the fire.

Again, I can't tell you how many, if any, fish were caught, but I can tell you this: the grub was good, the company better, we made no runs to the hospital, so I'd have to say that the fishing was excellent.

Nesbitts

It was the mid-to-late sixties, and I had just heard the rumor. It couldn't possibly be true. Then came confirmation on the radio. It was true all right, and I had a mission.

The Whiteside Theater and a local radio station were putting on an auction for kids. The gimmick? Instead of money, you could bid for new toys with Nesbitts bottle caps. Now nobody and I mean nobody, liked Nesbitts Orange Soda better than this kid right here. There were to be several auctions over the summer and I had heard from a very reliable source that one of the items to be auctioned off was a brand new bike. Money being short in those days, this seemed to be the perfect answer to a small boys dreams of buying a shiny new bike. This was in fact the only answer.

By the time the first auction had come and gone I had accrued only a few dozen caps. Rumor had it though, that the bike went for only one hundred and twenty five caps. Not out of the realm of possibility. My plan was to intensify my cap collecting, skip the next auction, and clean house at the final one. My plan and apparently everyone else's.

I looked every place that might have caps. I checked around the snack-shack at the bean field. I looked in the ditches for empties to trade in on full ones. And of course anytime I had a spare dime, I'd buy a cold one and pocket the cap. If I happened to be in town, I would look all over the parking lots and gutters in search of that bright orange cap.

I went into a gas station one day to buy a pop, and I saw a kid ask the attendant if he could have all the caps in the pop machine. I smacked myself on the head, cursing myself for not having thought of it first. It was the golden rule that the whole retail world revolves around. VOLUME CURES EVERYTHING!

So with that in mind I made daily rounds (within the eight-mile radius of my home) to every establishment that might sell Nesbitts soda. Preferring the ones that had the Nesbitts thermometer on the outside of the building, but I hit anyplace that offered hope. Not that many years ago most grocery stores had bottle openers attached to the check-stand. Underneath that opener was a metal cylinder that caught the caps. Opening pop bottles used to be a regular service to the customer. It was my intention to cash in on this cornucopia of caps.

The days turned into weeks and my stockpile of caps was only a couple of hundred strong. At the second auction the bike went for about six or seven hundred caps. I would recount my pile nightly but the numbers barely changed. Discouragement was settling in.

One night my brother in law Sam called, wanting to know if my brother Dan and I would like to go on a grain run with him to neighboring Washington State. As normal kids, this was a big deal for us. A chance to ride in an eighteen wheeler in the middle of the night to points unknown was high adventure at it's best.

We would leave early evening in order to get in line around midnight. Then depending on the weather, we would sleep in the cab of the truck, or on top of the grain in the back. I've slept in a lot of strange places over the years, but few are as comfortable as on top of a truckload of grain. When the sun would finally wake us up, they would start unloading that long line of trucks, which left Dan and I with a number of hours to kill. We would wander around looking for just the right amount of mischief to get into, find some invaluable treasures, and then head down to the river and snag carp.

It would finally be time for Sam to go and square up with the office on his load of grain. The three of us walked into the office and my eyes immediately focused on a pop machine. I timidly asked the big man behind the counter if I could have the caps in it. He grinned a little and led me down into the basement where he pointed to four cardboard boxes. I had struck the mother lode of bottle caps. It turned out to be between one and two gunnysacks worth of bottle caps, gunnysacks being a more familiar unit of measure in those days. Into the back of the eighteen wheeler they went, and down the road I went, with visions of grandeur dancing around in my head. The only thing I wasn't certain of was the ratio of Nesbitts versus duds.

The day of the final auction arrived, and so did about a hundred kids with grocery bags full of caps. I had mine crammed into an Avon suitcase. I couldn't spot anyone right away that appeared to have more than I. The crowd parted as I walked into the theater. Whether it was because they were in awe of the amount of caps I must've had in the suitcase, or they thought I was going to try to sell them Avon products, either way I was walking tall and there to do some business. I settled into the back row.

The bike was wheeled out on stage first and the bidding commenced. My heart was pounding but before I knew it, the bidding shot right past my twelve hundred plus caps, and just kept right on going. I couldn't believe it, someone must have gotten there before I did, with four, maybe five gunnysacks of caps. Heartbroken, I scanned the remaining prizes. I honed in on an A.M.-F.M. Transistor radio. It was a dandy, with a built in carrying strap and a neat little earphone. The bidding started and, at around three hundred,

I raised my hand. It brought back fond memories of being with my dad at the livestock auctions, the smell of popcorn being a darn sight better than the stockyards. I can even remember what my dad would tell us at those auctions. He'd say, *"The first one of you kids who raises his hand during bidding gets a whooping"*. He was probably kidding, although none of us kids were brave enough to find out.

The bidding continued, little kids folded, but I kept going. With reckless abandon I would outbid all others. 400,425,450 and up it went. At one point I'm sure I heard a gasp or two coming from some of the kids. *"Who was this stranger with the Avon suitcase, and where did he come from?"* This I was sure they were whispering to themselves. 550, 600,650, and on it went until it was just myself and one other kid. It was like a tennis match, with the crowd turning their heads back and forth to follow the bidding and to see if this kid with the suitcase would keep going.

This was my first encounter with what it must feel like to be wealthy. To have all the aces, to boldly go where this kid had never been before, or oddly enough gone since. I rode a lot of miles in search of those bottle caps. I got to know every gas station attendant and grocery clerk in my little corner of the world.

A couple of years ago my brother (and good friend) Dan, gave me an old Nesbitts bottle he found somewhere. That soda was the elixir of my youth. Their motto said it best. ***Nesbitts name on a soft drink, Is like Sterling stamped on silver.*** I have never had a better soda, nor been prouder of a radio, than the one I walked out of that theater with, so many years ago.

Gates

One of the problems with growing up in the wide-open spaces was all the confounded gates separating one wide-open space from the next. The big mystery to the bare-footers plodding down that dusty road, was why anyone would feel compelled to separate one field from the next, when both were owned by the same farmer.

A gate is no problem when you're on foot as you just scramble over it and continue on your way. A bike is another matter. You have to lean it against the gate, climb up and pull the bike to the top. There you must take aim and strategically hurl the bike over, taking note as to how many times it bounces before coming to a crooked wheeled rest. Anybody can make a bike bounce three times, but with careful aim, and by hitting both tires at the same time, you could sometimes attain five or more.

Our old man was always scratching his head at the overall poor condition of our bikes. He knew that none of these gates were locked, so the mere act of us throwing our bikes over the gate rather than opening it, just drove home the fact that while all of his boy's were exceptionally strong, none of them were particularly bright.

Taking a farm rig through a gate was always a bit of a chore since none of them had a parking gear or an emergency brake. As a matter of fact none of them had a battery strong enough to honk the horn that wasn't there, much less restart the engine. So if you were going to shut off the rig, you had to do it on a hill so you could roll it to a start the next time you needed it. And you had better start it with the first pop of the clutch or you would have to round up volunteers to help you push the rig back up the hill so you could make the attempt again. The volunteers generally frowned upon this sort of endeavor.

Taking a rig through a gate that was on an incline posed the biggest problem. We had developed a system that involved a series of really big rocks that we kept at strategic intervals alongside the road. You would drive up to the gate, hop off the rig, pick up the rock and jam it under the now rolling back tire. It was folly to jam the rock under the front tire since that usually just made the tire turn, usually towards you, and as you were running for your life the rig would roll off into a tree or worse yet the slough. After getting the rig stopped, you would open the gate, drive the rig through, go through the rock routine one more time, close the gate, and then drive off cussing the farmer for being to cheap to buy batteries.

Each rig posed different problems for this system of rocks. The worst rig to try and get through the gate would probably be a tractor pulling an irrigation pipe trailer. The reason being that the extra twenty five-foot of trailer would put you that much further through the gate. So you'd hop off the tractor only to discover that you were now twenty-five critical feet past the nearest big rock. At this point you would take a deep breath, hop off the tractor, run and grab the big rock, and run back towards the now rolling tractor, the trip back being much shorter since the rolling tractor would meet you halfway. Then you had to jam the big rock under the big back tire. Normally that would stop it, although sometimes the tractor would pick up enough speed to go right over the rock. When this would happen you'd have to wait for the back tire to get done running over it and then grab it before the front tire had it's turn, and then re-jam it under the back tire.

At this point you notice two things. The first being that

you had just successfully stopped a huge tractor by jamming a rock under a back tire that was almost twice as tall as you were. The second thing you notice is that during all this rock shuffling, the rig has rolled backwards far enough that the trailer is now halfway through the gate. Now you

would have to start completely over, which usually gave you ample time and reason, to once again, cuss the farmer for his aversion towards batteries.

There was always the element of risk of getting run over by those tires you were jamming rocks under. Every year or so, someone we all knew would die from a tractor accident. And whenever it happened, the word crushed was usually very prominently used. Now I could live with getting crushed under a John Deere, but there was serious hell to pay if the tractor rolled backwards and into a farmer's gate.

It's not that farmers are particularly proud of their gates, they're just expensive and a nuisance to hang. So mid-size boys learn fast not to crush them. Oh you could bow them once and a while, but for god sakes don't tear them off of the hinges. When your only making a dollar an hour the hard way, the last thing you want to spend a half a months pay on is a lousy gate. Although the whole time your hanging that gate, it does give you ample time to ponder on the farmers allergic reaction to the notion of buying batteries.

Basketball Abuse

The old man had decided that his four boys needed a basketball hoop. So he rounded up some re-bar from work, welded it into a circle, mounted it to some plywood, and stuck it on a post out by the round corral. Our court was a truckload of sawdust, and the net was made from a gunnysack. I asked my mom why we couldn't afford a real net. She'd say *"Now Billy, just think of all the poor people out there who don't even have gunny-sacks."* Well this line of reasoning really threw me, mostly because of the fact that my name was Dave.

Some of the many problems with a sawdust basketball court in Oregon, is that it is always wet, you can't really dribble, and every other time you shoot the ball, you'd get sawdust in your eyes, which really smarts. I'd go running into the house, screaming like a banshee, and my mom would ever so gently get the sawdust out of my eye, give me a hug, and then say something like *"There you go Jimmy, now go back outside and play."* This gave me a warm feeling, because my brother's name was Jim, so I knew she was honing in on which one I was.

Looking back on it all, this could only be described as one lousy basketball court. One of the worst parts came whenever someone would shoot an air ball and it would land in the ditch behind the backboard. The ditch was comprised of rotten sawdust, and of course the things that take place in round corrals and horse-stalls. This bacterial experiment can only be described as a really thick, black, stinky liquid. Quite often as not, when the ball would land in this ooze, the game would be over. The ball would sometimes sit in the ditch for days and days. Eventually one of us would pull it out, and wash it off, being careful not to get any of the ooze on you, since it was strong enough to eat through rawhide. What we had now was a ball that was half-orange and half-black. Nowadays you have to pay extra for a multi-colored ball. We not only invented the look, but ours had a fragrance factor that was beyond description.

One day found my kid brother Dan, and myself, playing basketball wars. The rules were simple enough, you just chase each other around and try to inflict as much pain as possible on the opponent, by hitting them with the ball. At one point in the game I had cornered Dan up on top the chicken shed. When duck hunting, you are supposed to take your shots while they are in flight, not while they are just sitting in the water. In basketball wars there were no rules against sluicing someone while on top of a chicken shed. My strategy at this point was to hit him so hard, that it would knock him off the roof and into the neighbor's pasture. I wound up, and threw with all my might, but instead of knocking him off, he caught the ball. I went into a full-scale panic. Dan was famous through out the county for his deadly aim.

There wasn't any time to run, so I dropped to the ground and assumed the fetal position. I lay there waiting for the stinging pain that was about to arrive on my now exposed back. After about a minute of waiting, with no ball hitting myself, or even close, I warily looked towards the shed. Dan was nowhere to be seen. Cautiously, I approached the shed, where I discovered what had taken place. When Dan had gone for his wind up, just like the baseball pitchers do on TV, he had been standing so close to the edge of the roof, that he planted his left foot into thin air, and fell the ten feet to what appeared to be his untimely death.

I looked down at him and he was just lying there still clutching the ball. I did what all small boy's do when approaching a dead animal. I poked him in the ribs with a two-foot stick. Now at this point I have to explain kid logic. When approaching a dead animal, and poking him with a stick, you are given a runaway time of approximately one-second per foot of stick, in case they are still alive. On retrospect, I should have poked my kid brother with about a twelve-foot stick.

Temper, Temper

"AND ANOTHER THING, I'M SICK AND TIRED OF YOU ALWAYS PICKIN ON ME AND DAVE! SO WHY DON' T YOU JUST LEAVE US ALONE, AND PICK ON SOMEONE YOUR OWN SIZE!"

Brother Dan was five, I was six, and he had just given the big guy a piece of his mind. I wanted to cheer him on, but froze in terror instead. Jim and Doug, our two older brothers, who had also witnessed the confrontation, just stood there in silent disbelief.

My whole family had short fuses, but that day just happened to be Dan's turn. He suddenly realized he was outmatched, would get no help from his brothers, and in all probability was about to die. He had lost his temper with his own father, and thirty years ago, fathers did not find this behavior cute.

My dad had these incredible blue eyes that when lit up, could destroy things in its path, not unlike today's laser beams. Dan saw the beams heading his way, and took off on a dead run. Chunks of sod were flying behind him, caused either by his shoes or the laser beams. My dad eventually caught him, and drug him out to the shed. My brothers and I solemnly went into the house to prepare for the funeral.

Our house was the recipient of many lost tempers during my childhood. Friends would stop by and puzzle over why we'd have outdated feedstore calendars hanging at sporadic heights all through the house, until they would lift them and discover a hole that had been kicked in the wall by some hot tempered little foot.

Some years later found me having trouble keeping my dune buggy running. After about six hours of knuckle bustin mechanicking, the dune buggy would still not run. I tried one last trick. I grabbed the windshield, shook it rather firmly, and shouted something to Mr.Goodwrench in the sky. This technique quite often will help with carburation problems, but this time, only shattered my windshield.

Three years later, at "The Hardly Runnin Ranch" outside of Ignacio, Colorado, my bride and I were having a calm marital debate. We were having it in our car at two a.m., so as not to wake the whole house up. At one point in the conversation, I tapped the windshield with my fist, which shattered instantly. Clearly a defective windshield was at fault here, but I think you can guess who lost her temper, and blamed me for the whole incident.

One time when I was little, I had a top that would spin for everybody but me. It too was obviously defective and quite possibly possessed, so I took my little ax to it. It must also have been very cold that day, because I also set fire to it.

I would like this new computer to think about this previous paragraph very carefully.

Swimmin Holes

I was fortunate enough to grow up in a family whose income could not justify many things. There were more kids than paycheck, so my folks gave us many things that money couldn't buy. Among those things were literally dozens and dozens of swimmin holes. It was the cheapest, best entertainment out there. It seemed like no matter where we went one of us would find a swimmin hole. I often thought that if my family had been on a plane that crashed in the middle of a desert, one of us would find a swimmin hole within ten minutes or less.

We swam in rivers, streams, creeks, lakes, ponds, gravel pits, sloughs, and even a ditch or two. We stopped just short of mill and settling ponds. Okay, Okay, maybe a few millponds, but we never swam in settling ponds. All right, maybe once, but I'm sure it was a really hot day.

Clear water on the other hand, meant one thing and one thing only. Somehow you had to find a mud bog, (or build your own) and get as muddy as humanly possible. Then you would run as fast as your muddy little legs would carry you and shallow dive into the water, leaving a glorious mud slick following you much like the vapor trail behind a jet.

Each swimmin hole posed it's own form of adventure, especially for youngsters with an over active imagination. Lakes would become oceans, chock full of sea serpents. Creeks would become raging rivers, and the little sticks you would send down them, became settlers on boats, battling the River of No Return. (And swear to god, the settlers never returned!)

Ponds had a particularly eerie sense about them. I think it came from the fact that the murkier the water, the less you can see, therefore, the more monsters that can live there. Monsters hate clear water. Don't ask me how I know, I just know. Just because you've never seen a baby hummingbird, doesn't mean they don't exist.

Since you can't open your eyes in murky water, you are left with feeling your way around the bottom with your feet. Oddly enough, when you step on something sharp, (even when it's sharp enough to cut your foot) deep down you know that this is not some monsters teeth. It's when you step on something really ookie that you begin to panic. Because you know it is the monster's leg, tentacle, or worse case scenario, his tongue. Now if you are unfortunate enough to step on his tongue, I'll be honest with you, you're a goner. I can't think of a single relative or friend who stepped on a monster's tongue and lived to tell about it.

One summer in particular, we lost a farmer that we all knew real well. He'd flipped his tractor into the river and they found his tractor but not him. This whole scenario made swimming around that area extremely uncomfortable. Every time you'd see something kind of pale, down deep in the water, or you would step on something kind of ookie, odds are you would fly out of that river like your butt was on fire, and take off running down the road or across the field, yelling at the top of your lungs " *I found Elmer! I found Elmer!*" I think realistically, we found Elmer on the average of about ten to twelve times a week that summer.

Rope swings and rafts were key ingredients to any swimming hole. First you had to appropriate (steal) the rope from someone you knew, who obviously didn't need it anymore. You can tell when someone doesn't need it anymore because they usually just leave it lying around. This rule also applies to building materials and tools. Ideally the raft would be made from anything within a half mile of the hole. We built a log raft one time that would have made Tom Sawyer green with envy. We had it anchored to the bottom of the river with rock-filled gunnysacks. It lasted most of the summer, and then one day, off down the river she went. We never did find her.

One rope swing we had was just incredible. It had a series of knots in it for hand holds and a great big knot the size of a cantaloupe at it's base for sitting or standing on. It went way out over the river, especially if you climbed way up on this windfall to take off from.

One summer day found a bunch of us skinny dipping at that swimmin hole, and I decided to take off from the highest point on the rope swing that I could reach. Through all the excitement of attaining new world records on rope swinging, I failed to notice that when I swung out over the river, the excess rope that should have been swinging **at** my side had somehow found its way **between** my legs. I turned loose of the rope once I was out over the river and the trailing eight to ten feet of rope started removing the hide from between my legs as I fell. This was extremely painful but not nearly as painful as hitting the knots one at a time on the way down, particularly the cantaloupe knot at the bottom.

I don't remember much after that, although my kid brother said that when I hit the **BIG** knot at the bottom of the rope, it changed my direction enough to make me do a double back flip into the river. He kept telling me what a great flip it was as I was making that long, six-mile, bowlegged journey home.

Skinny-dippin

I grew up in a time and a place where skinny-dipping was more functional than fashionable. We were always near water, and you didn't always have cut-offs handy. So when the day was hot, and the water called, you'd answer. Oh sure, sometimes it would call at night, and on rare occasions it would call in the winter, but the important thing was to answer the call. When your farming all day and your work takes you by some cool water, I defy anyone to ignore the call. I have answered it regularly during each decade of the last half of this century, and with any luck, will continue right on into the next.

There are many hazards that come with skinny-dipping. There is always the odd splinter picked up while climbing a tree to dive from, and a 16 penny nail sticking out of a homemade raft will most certainly <u>seize</u> your attention, if not something else. Rope swings dangling <u>between</u> your legs instead of <u>beside</u> your legs can tear off enough hide to make a boy wonder if he'll ever be able to ride a bike again. (And let me tell you, that's one tough horse to climb back onto). Biting insects like nothing better than a fresh batch of tender vittles on the menu, and they don't seem to care that it's only the child's portion either. You have to be real careful swatting at them with a stick, since the scream you let out from missing the insect and hitting your <u>very existence</u>, will echo far longer than the scream from the bug's bite itself.

There is also a certain apprehension when skinny-dipping with your own gender, but cold water is a great equalizer, and from that point on you can just commence having fun. There are no rules of etiquette to worry about, which is always nice. And you don't have to make idle chitchat over where you got your suit. Oh, every once in a while it's acceptable to say, " *Boy **that** sunburn has got to hurt*!" or " *What the hell kind of scar is that anyway*!" But that's about all. Laughter or a round of applause is probably the only social faux pas that you could commit.

Having skinny-dipped both oceans and hundreds of spots in between on this great continent, I'd have to say that it's about the same all over, although the Atlantic is a far cry warmer than the Pacific. The Atlantic also has a fair amount of pesky fish that bump into you, which tends to get the heart pumping.

I spent a couple of weeks on a beach in South Carolina hunting sharks teeth at low tide, and it never once occurred to me that where you find teeth, you might also find the owner. I hadn't seen **Jaw's** yet, which was probably just as well. Paranoia and skinny- dipping go hand in hand, with or without sharks present. Also, as long as we are on the subject, skinny-dipping in the Atlantic during an electrical storm can only be described as (now what's that word that rhymes with cupid? Oh yes) exhilarating!

Skinny-dipping today is about the same as it was in the fifties and sixties, except for two things: There is probably legislation against it now, and back then there wasn't the threat of video cameras, with or without a zoom lens. In the seventies there was a whole shift in thinking that sent a big chunk of the population skinny-dipping. But an awful lot of those people went only because they read somewhere that they had to. It settled down in the eighties when the throng became decaffeinated. So here we sit in the nineties and that same throng can't decide whether it would be politically correct to skinny-dip, much less where they would put their pager. I have a few ideas, but once again, remain silent.

I would have to say that the best years for skinny-dipping for myself were probably the sixties. I didn't know about counter-cultures, drugs, racial tensions, youth movements, or bucking the establishment. About all I did know, was that after twelve hours of buckin hay on a hot summer's day, nothing felt better than rippin off your britches and goin skinny dippin. And it still holds true today.

Guilty

The CPR (Child to Parent Ratio) in our house was five to two. My parents had five kids over a span of seven or eight years. All parents reading this think very carefully about this last line. I'm talking a new kid every year and a half, during just under two presidential terms. As a single father of three boy's, I find myself understanding more about my folks everyday. They both worked many jobs trying to keep food on the table, so anything resembling rest was just not a part of their regime. My folks also had one other strike going against them. Their kids were some of the strangest, orneriest, rambunctious, evil, hell bent for leather, passle of young-ins to hit town in quite a while. I would like to say however, that we came by it honestly. (My boys coincidentally, say the very same thing)

In the last part of the fifties, we moved to a little place out in the country. I often suspected that we moved not so much for the peace and tranquillity of country life, but probably because the city wanted us kids out of town. Kind of a " *The chickens and other critters can stay, but the kids have to go*" scenario. It was almost as if we were guilty without a chance of being proven innocent. Looking back on it all, since it was a big event for us to watch our dad cut the heads off those same chickens, it was with a great sense of relief that when he did move, he took both the chickens and us kids. Thank God there was room, because I have a pretty good idea which of us he'd have left behind if there hadn't been.

Granted, we had our share of mishaps. There were a certain amount of fires, but no buildings were ever lost. Well actually, we lost a barn and a couple of horse stalls one night, but fortunately we had a once in a lifetime perfect alibi. All of us boy's were in town with our folks at the time of the big fire. My sister Linda was out on a field burn when one of the farmers came up to her and said *"You know, you sure look purty when the fields on fire, and by the way, so is your folk's house."* Linda knew he wasn't kidding because most farmers just don't joke much. I don't know why they don't, I just know they don't. Anyway she hopped in the closest rig to drive home (That's how it was in those day's, all rigs were up for grabs, since everybody knew everybody, and keys were always left in the ignition.) The problem was that this was a newer rig with a lot of fancy buttons, and in the process of trying to turn on the headlights she kept popping the hood and the trunk open, and god knows the windshield washers worked just fine, and all the bells and buzzers added a nice ambiance, but they were really starting to tick her off. Anyway, Linda got to our house somehow, in spite of all the buttons.

We were a mile or so from home, when we noticed the fire trucks heading back into town. One of us boys made a comment about how it would be funny if they were coming from our house. Mom shuddered, and Dad, who was a quiet man, somehow got even quieter. I think he uttered (UH-OH) when he noticed the muddy tracks leaving our driveway and onto the highway. Linda was there when our car finally stopped in front of our house, which was unscathed. A couple of barns behind the house however, were large piles of glowing embers.

The fire dept. blamed the electric fence for the fire, which naturally brought on some telepathic high-five's between my brothers and I. Our old man, doing his own bit of telepathy, looked at us as if to say " *I don't know how you pulled this one off, but it better not happen again*." I was thinking to myself " *Heck, how could it happen again, the barns gone for cryin out loud!"* I remained silent. The main reason I am alive today, was my steadfast rule of remaining silent around the old man.

There was also some occasional gunfire, although technically, we never really shot at one another, so much as sometimes we would shoot <u>towards</u> one another. There is quite a difference believe it or not. When you shoot <u>at</u> someone, you assume you are going to hit them, but when you shoot <u>towards</u> someone, you assume you are going to get their attention, but you're pretty sure your not going to hit them. I can only imagine the kind of whooping I would have got if I had hit one of my siblings, instead of just coming close.

One year we went on a vacation down to Tijuana. We stayed with my mom's brother Shorty, a retired jockey. My older brother Doug had bought a cute little switchblade knife while we were across the border. It was because of that knife, that the most memorable parts of the trip were <u>not</u> all the neat places we visited, which were quite a few, the most vivid parts of that trip were the periodic stabbing that he would inflict upon us, all the way back to Oregon. That was beyond a shadow of a doubt one of the longest trips of my life. There I was, eight, maybe nine years old, and every time I would get close to dosing off ....Wham! I'd get stabbed in the butt with Doug's switchblade. My folks, hearing the scream, would shout towards the back of the truck " **Knock it off**!" Well just how in the heck was I supposed to knock off getting stabbed in the butt with Doug's knife! Once again, I remained silent. Doug even kept his snickering muffled.

My dad had built a plywood deck in the back of this old Chevy panel truck, and that was where we rode to

Tijuana and back. There would be an ever-changing pile of kids, parents, blankets, and pillows on this plywood deck at any given time. When the old man hit the road, he put miles behind him. I have to tip my hat to him now though, he took us to more parts of the country in more rigs that shouldn't have left the driveway, much less the state, but he always got us home. He was of a special breed. I see him a lot in each of my siblings, but I see him the most in my kid brother. I tip my hat to them both.

We five kids were a curious lot, who liked to push buttons <u>because</u> they were there, rather than read the instructions as to <u>why</u> they were there. My folks taught us to both build fires and to put them out. If there was a line, we crossed it. If there was a door, we opened it. If it was locked, then we went in through the window. If something couldn't be done, we found a way to do it anyway. We pulled many triggers, but felt all repercussions. We were a frisky bunch who kept our folks on their toes. For years, while at work, every time my mom would hear a siren, she would cringe. She just knew it was heading to our house, and more than once it did.

Which I suppose is why, periodically when my folks would get home, and the five of us kids would be sitting on the couch, with those angelic looks on our faces, my folks would just say ***"Let the whoopings commence*****!"** You see, my parents knew that at any given time, at least half of us were guilty of something, and we probably had a good whooping coming anyway. And of course we usually did.

Doors

We were raised in the country, and it seemed like everybody we knew, had between two hundred and two thousands acres. We had just under two, and managed to fill up every square inch of both of them. We raised dozens and dozens of animals, ranging from hogs, horses, cows, chickens, turtles, turkeys, pheasant, rabbits, two wild fox, the meanest spider monkey to ever walk the face of the earth, and one baby alligator that would never reach skinning size.

While in the Air Force, my oldest brother Jim, came across a guy with a bear for sale. That was one of the few times the old man said no. The horses we rode, but most of the other critters were destined for the kitchen. There was no room for weak stomachs at our table.

Naturally it didn't take long for five kids to outgrow two acres, and once we did, we of course set our sights on all neighboring farms. We went to work for each one of them, which was of course the farmer's eventual undoing. Under the pretense of employment, we would then settle in like fleas on a black lab and no amount of scratching could get us off. But with all due respect, where as the farmers couldn't get rid of us, nor could we get rid of the farmers.

It wasn't until many years later, when I started to get acquainted with some town kids, that I discovered that it was common practice for a lot of people to lock their doors. We never did, nor did anybody we knew. For most of my childhood, there was no key to be found for our house. The rare times that we would lock the door were when we left town for a few days, and even then, upon returning home, it was up to one of us kids to go in through the unlocked back door and go unlock the front. If we were leaving the state, we'd lock both doors, and upon returning, one of us would go in through a window.

The down side to not locking doors is that you might be taking a nap, or contemplating the universe in the bathroom, when suddenly you'd hear the front door open and shut, and some farmer would holler " ANYBODY HOME?" And you better holler back, because the farmer not only wouldn't knock, he'd just keep wandering around till he found who or what he was looking for.

Our favorite farm was one or two thousand acres in size. It had a couple of sloughs, two rivers, and several gravel ponds for swimming, fishing and camping. We would sometimes camp there for days, going home only to steal food and say "Hi" to the folks. This farm also had an abundance of deer, grouse, pheasant, duck, geese, nutria, and other creatures, for our hunting pleasure.

Every day offered much adventure as you never really knew how it would wind up. You might be training bean plants in the morning, bucking hay in the afternoon, and by evening you'd have hitched a ride on a grain truck heading for Washington. The course of each day was a continual spin of the agricultural roulette wheel and you never knew where it would land.

One day we were changing irrigation pipe, when a light bulb went off over one of our heads. This so startled the rest of the group, that they quickly grabbed rocks and sticks to beat to death that same person. It wasn't until we realized that the light bulb merely meant that he had just had an idea that we put our weapons down and listened to his plan. That night after work, carrying our sleeping bags and a rucksack of food, we forded the Long Tom River, to camp on a little island in the middle. As it was more of a gravel spit than an actual island, it was much like sleeping on golf balls. We fell asleep though, with full bellies under a full moon, listening to the sounds of the wind whistling through the willows. The river trickled past us on both sides, carrying all of our worries away with it on its journey to the Columbia.

We awoke the next morning, not to an alarm clock, nor a rooster. We awoke under a herd of dairy cows that had forded the river at first light. Dairy cows aren't the prettiest of sights on a good day, but they take on a whole different perspective when you're poking your head out of a sleeping bag and looking up at the business end of a fertilizer factory.

But of course that is what makes an adventure, an adventure. You fall asleep on one side of the door, not knowing what awaits you on the other upon awakening. When you reach a point in your life that you do know what is on the other side of the door, you have to ask yourself, what the point of going through it is. It is the unknown that compels the soul. It also makes you stand just a tad taller, smell a bit deeper, and listen just a little harder. It is the unknown that makes you realize the excitement of having all your cards laid out in front of you. When there is no point in bluffing, since your standing there buck naked, with obviously nothing up your sleeve. It is at this point that the pressure is both off, and on. It is at this point that the journey begins.

When I turned thirty, I quit my job, loaded my wife, my two-year-old son, and two dogs into a small pick-up with a homemade canopy and drove to Alaska. Shortly after seeing the Northern Lights for the first time, we discovered that what lay on the other side of that Arctic door, was son number two. So there we were in a small cabin, with two light bulbs, no running water, a small boy on the floor and one in the oven, no job, and a wife who was not too keen on the idea of having to use an outhouse for the duration of the pregnancy. Hanging on that outhouse was the only door that I knew what lay on the other side of.

Last month I awoke to discover that I had turned forty, lost a wife a few doors back, can't jump as high as I used to, and was heading towards being bald. But I do have three fine sons helping me bust through doors now. We still never know what lies on the other side, and occasionally we have to re-hang a door or two, but we still keep going through. And thus the adventure continues.

Sauna's

There is nothing to me quite like the smell of cedar. And there is nothing quite like the smell of cedar walls and benches inside of a sauna. They are an odiferous delight. The heat enhances the smell, and fortunately the cedar absorbs (and kills) all else that you may not want to smell. Isn't that great?

The components of a sauna are fairly simple. You need a hot cedar box about half the size of your average bedroom. Some of the more professional ones are about the same size of your average bedroom. Although, some of my bedrooms have been about half the size of a small sauna. As a matter of fact, I built a sauna once, which was about one-eighth the size of a small bedroom. Let's see now, if half a sauna left Pittsburgh and met a train going sixty miles per hour from Jacksonville........? Wait a minute, I'm rambling, now where was I, in a really small bedroom, or a really huge sauna? Well it's a moot point, since there are times when they both smell the same.

A man named Platt owned the first sauna I ever went into. I'm not too sure on the spelling, but it is phonetically correct. Platt is a very difficult name to mispronounce. And lets be honest for a minute, aren't you just a little bit glad, that you don't have Platt as a last name? But once again I digress.........

Just outside of the sauna, was a cast iron-bathtub that he would fill with a garden hose. Once it was filled with water, he would put in several blocks of ice. During the sauna, when you had sweat what you were sure was your last drop, and your lungs felt like they were on fire, you would get up and exit the room, to a chorus of <u>SHUT THE DOOR!</u> and slide into the tub of ice water. This is quite an experience.

Eventually my dad gave in to all his boy's hounding on wanting a sauna of their own. Fortunately for us, if there was one thing the old man loved to do, it was build things. And the only thing better than building things brand new, was the challenge of building things out of what was lying around. Well the biggest thing lying around back then, was our nasty old abandoned chicken coop. But after a lot of shoveling, a few panels of particle board, and a retired Ashley wood-stove, we had us a first class sauna. Oh sure, there were some snobby types that would ask, "Just what kind of chicken sh_t sauna is this!" To which we would reply "Just how many kinds of chicken sh_t saunas do you think there are?" I do love a snappy, country debate. I never win em, but I do love em.

Anyway, we had what we considered a fairly first class sauna. We would crank up the wood-stove, and sit there and sweat, thinking about how many chickens had been raised in that hot box, to eventually grace our dinner table. We also tried to come up with an answer as to why it didn't smell quite like all the other saunas, but before we could put our finger on it, it would be hot enough to exit once again to a chorus of <u>SHUT THE DOOR</u>! Since we didn't have a spare bathtub or watering trough to dip into, we would just turn the hose on ourselves. Although a couple of times we were blessed with snow on the ground, so we would just roll around naked in it, and then lay there looking up at the stars. What a wonderfully simple time.

A few years later found me in a sauna in a ritzy house in Connecticut during a hitchhiking sojourn. Hot is hot, and the smell of cedar is virtually the same regardless of your economic or social status. I don't know what the heck I was doing there, since I had absolutely no economic <u>or</u> social status. But I did notice one big difference. When you reached the saturation point of heat and you chose to leave the sauna, once again to a chorus of <u>SHUT THE</u> <u>DOOR!</u> , Instead of sliding into a tub of ice-water, or turning the hose on yourself, we got to break through the ice and dive into their swimming pool. Now let me tell you, diving into an icy pool is a far cry easier than sliding slowly into a bathtub filled with ice cubes.

Many years later, while I was living in the Sierra Nevada's, my brother Doug showed me how to make a sweat lodge out of willow saplings and visquene. He had picked up this technique from some Indians somewhere during his twenty years of hitchhiking. (Doug has enough miles on his thumb to qualify for several Toyota commercials) It was a simple dome design about four feet tall at the center and six feet in diameter. It cost only ten bucks to make, but was strong enough to withstand several winters and more than a few blizzards.

There was no shouting of <u>SHUT THE DOOR!</u> Since it didn't really have one. You had to crawl in through a flap on your hands and knees. It was heated by lava rock that I baked in the fireplace of the small cabin we lived in and then placed in a small hole I dug in the center of the sweat lodge. There were no cedar benches to sit on so we parked our butts on the dirt floor.

I have been in many saunas in many states. But I have to say that short of a very special chicken coop in Oregon, there is nothing quite like sitting in a homemade sauna at the five thousand foot level of some of the prettiest mountains on earth, with the nearest light being that of the moon peeking through an aging cedar forest.

Timber

One of my earliest recollections is that of the word timber. Actually it was more like **TIMBER!** My Mom, in her eternal quest for trying to help put food on the table and simultaneously keep track of her five young-uns, had hauled her evil horde up into the high country in search of pinecones. A cone buyer would buy pinecones for the seed. On this particular trip she brought her best friend and her two daughters. The nine of us were piled into our aging V.W. bus and we kids knew we were in search of pinecones and maybe some Chittum bark. Chittum bark fetched a good price due to its natural laxative powers. It didn't seem important to me at the time, as I was only five years old and a healthy bundle of Chittum in my own dang right.

The most terrifying word I had ever heard at that point in my life was the word **TIMBER!** Between my mom, and my evil older brothers and sister, they had impressed upon me the dangers of pinecone hunting in logging country. The biggest danger was being that of hearing the word **TIMBER!** And then moments later wearing a hundred-foot pine tree for a blanket.

Somehow my mom had managed to get all of us into a stand of tall trees that were being logged. And I don't mean being logged yesterday, or even that morning, I mean they were being logged all around us. There were a lot of men running around with chain saws, who seemed to enjoy all of the critters, that mom had brought into the forest. The pickins were a lot easier because of mom getting us into the thick of it. As the big trees would fall, and shortly after the ground would stop shaking, there would be a covey of kids scurrying all over the big fallen trees in search of pine cones. Some of the kids managed to find squirrels caches during the search, which produced an abundance of the treasured pinecones.

The two main dilemmas's with this invasion into the forest were pitch and poison oak. Seven kids running around like farts in a skillet had managed to find probably as much pitch as pinecones. We were covered from head to toe, which we knew meant a turpentine spit bath when we got home.

My kid brother Dan, came home covered in pitch and poison oak. The poison oak spread so badly that it covered most of his four-year-old body. All he could do was lie naked on the couch, with a hand towel over his privates. He looked kind of like a Picasso version of the Energizer Bunny. I hope he doesn't read this, because that last line is probably gonna get this forty year old yet another one of his whooping's.

My mom did anything she could to ease the pressure of my dad's overloaded life, as if her tending to their five kids wasn't enough. My dad was in a lot of pain and out of work, while recuperating from a broken back from the sawmill. So if she could find a dollar for gas and figure out a way to make seventy five cent's worth of grub feed a party of nine, while spending a day in the woods collecting two and a half dollars worth of pine cones, the family was six bits ahead no matter how you looked at it. Thanks to her, and a goat or two along the way, her busted-up mill worker husband was able to keep a family of seven fed. By the way, my dad, nor the rest of us for that matter, ever knew we were eating goat. You see my mom was, and still is, an incredible cook. She is also the only person I have ever met who actually could make a silk purse out of a sow's ear.

Never say "It can't be done" within earshot of my mom.

Many years later found me in living in the Sierra-Nevada Mountains. I spent most of my time off from work either gold panning or cutting firewood for the harsh winters we'd get in the high country. I cut and burnt twelve cords of wood during the winter of 79 alone. It wasn't unusual to go through three to four wheelbarrows of wood a day, and this was for a very small cabin.

One day I was cutting wood in the forest about a mile behind the cabin, when I stumbled onto a tree that was snapped in two by a recent storm. The top half had already been cut-up by someone else, but the bottom half was still standing and I decided to fall it. I parked my old Willys pick-up where I thought it would be out of harms way. I made the appropriate cuts on the tree but made two critical mistakes. One; I plain and simply cut it wrong, And Two; I forgot to yell **TIMBER!**

Since my Willys pick-up was one of the forefather's of all modern pick-ups, it was understandable that it was not only slow and cantankerous, but was also hard of hearing, so it probably wouldn't have moved out of the path of the falling tree even if it had wanted to.

To this day I can still hear and smell the big saws at work. There is something both frightening and exciting about, the snapping of branches, the ground shaking under your feet as the big trees come crashing down, while the loud cry of **TIMBER!** is still echoing through a young boy's ears.

There is so much noise that you are constantly looking around, positive that the crashing you are hearing will soon be your last. It is kind of ominous to be close enough to big saws and big trees that you can smell hear and <u>feel</u>, but you cannot always see. If you've never done it, you really should. And for a little added spice, try keeping an eye on seven kids during this experience.

Etiquette

Etiquette, much like beauty, is in the eye of the beholder. These are changing times and since I had no etiquette back in simpler days, I won't try to lay claim to any during these. I have performed what can be considered correct protocol at various moments in my life, but these were more of an instinctive reaction, rather than a socially correct choice. I've been living this way for forty years, so it must be OK. And even if it isn't, why change now? I may not know which fork to use while eating *vichyssoise,* but I get the job done.

Well maybe not, since during my research on how to spell *vichyssoise,* I remembered that it is eaten with a spoon. *Dang.*

SILVER-WARE

I knew a farmer who used one spoon and one spoon only for eating everything. It was a big spoon and he had used it for so many decades that it had worn down on the left side, to the point that it was sharp enough to cut meat. He used it in place of knife and fork, for breakfast, lunch, dinner and dessert. Very efficient if you think about it. He had nine boys and each knew not to touch the old man's spoon. They lived in a huge old farmhouse, and they all worked the big farm sun-up til sundown, seven days a week, year round.

He was pretty efficient with his wardrobe also. He had his work overalls, and than he had a good pair of Sunday go to meetin/funeral overalls. Considering how much food he put on America's table in the last seventy-five years, I would love to see some **scud** (socially correct underworked **d**o-gooder) attempt to explain silverware settings to this man. Of course they'd have never made it past the front door to begin with much less been invited in to eat, since they were fairly easy to spot. Every one in the county, who even slightly knew the farmer, also knew to just walk in through the kitchen door. Trouble however, generally knocks at the front door.

HUNTING
When hunting you should never offer advice on gutting a deer, unless specifically asked. About all you can do is just stand there and say " *Boy that's a dandy*!" Even if it isn't. You can be the first one to get to the deer, but you should never touch it before the one who shot it has. Never offer the use of your knife unless asked, even if the poor soul is wearing their elbow out trying to saw through what they should be slicing. It is the shooter's moment in the sun, so let him, or her, bask. Never compare any fallen prey, to any past trophies. The best trophy is the one at your feet, not the ones on your wall.

SKINNY-DIPPING
When skinny-dipping, never stare. That pretty much covers it.

CAMPING
When camping, burping and breaking wind are of no surprise to anyone, although it is in good form to ease into the latter. Your <u>natural</u> surroundings tend to bring out this external venting however, it should be of a <u>natural</u> velocity. Never force the issue, unless specifically requested. But remember it is always dangerous to put too much powder in any gun. It is also polite to respect your camping neighbor's

air space. If however you are camping with no neighbors, than it's pretty much a no holds barred situation. If the local forest creatures start throwing pinecones at you, then you have obviously crossed over the line.

One time during a motorcycle camping trip (involving a lot of beer and red hot sausages) we crossed so far over the line that the little forest creatures just packed their nuts, and moved to a different forest. Coincidentally, the hole in the ozone got a little larger that summer. Proper etiquette requires an apology during such incidents. (I did, and still do)

HITCH-HIKING

When hitch-hiking, and you come across a fellow thumb rider, always say or just nod a " Howdy", and then continue walking at least fifty yards beyond his spot. He was there first, and accordingly should have first crack at the next ride. When he does get his ride and he passes you by, it is good form to give him a congratulatory nod. Deep down you know that if he could, he'd give you a ride also. When a rig does pull over to give you a ride, <u>run</u> to meet it. Walking shows indifference, while running shows great appreciation on your part. Running, screaming and flailing your arms wildly about however will get you left in the dust. Try to contain your excitement.

After you've been picked up, keep your conversation light, and show a great interest in what your driver has to say. In the mid-seventies I got a ride from a guy somewhere in Nebraska. He was wearing camouflage clothing, was kind of skittish, and the inside of his rig smelled of smoke that had not come from traditional tobacco. After about an hour of really loud 60's music, and some particularly strange conversation, I asked him what the leather thing was that I had been watching dangle from his rear-view mirror. He answered by asking me if I knew anything about guns. This response confused me, but I told him I'd done my share of hunting and knew my way around most weapons. He then pointed behind the bucket seats we were riding on.

From my vantagepoint I could see, the unmistakable sight of a breather pipe on the barrel, of what was a military issue M-16 rifle. The breather pipe was to help keep the barrel a little cooler during fully automatic operation. I remained as calm as could be expected, (knowing fully well that this was even more illegal to own then those skinny cigarettes he'd been chain smoking) and inquired as to how he had managed to acquire such a magnificent piece of weaponry. He turned to me, pointing to an empty eye socket, and said "*I lost **this** in Vietnam, So I took **that** in return*", pointing again to the rifle. As it turns out, what I had been watching dangle from the mirror, was his eye patch.

Since he didn't suggest using me for a jackrabbit on that barren stretch of road, I can only assume I passed the etiquette test for that day. God only knows what might have happened however, if I had asked him which utensil he used for eating *vichyssoise*!

Semi-fast Food

I grew up in a time when we were just leaving the age of cafe's and drive-ins and just entering the age of fast food establishments. There was a time when I had never heard of Kentucky Fried Chicken, McDonalds or anything resembling a Taco Bell. The closest thing we had to quick cuisine were a few privately owned drive-in restaurants, including an A&W. My favorite's were the ones that had the girls delivering the trays of food on roller skates. It was a sight to behold for males of all ages.

You got to place your order through speakers, not unlike today's fast food places. The difference was that each parking space had it's own speaker. You also had to wait thirty to forty minutes for your order to get cooked and then hopefully find it's way to your car. My folk's car was a VW bus they had bought in the 50's. The embarrassing part about this car (besides the fact that it was two shades of goose-terd green) was that it's windows slid sideways rather than rolling up and down. Because of this, the roller skating cutie that delivered your tray, had to stand there and wait for you to unload this mountain of food and drink for seven, rather than attach it to your rolled down window, allowing you to unload it casually, like the rest of the cars in the parking lot, and coincidentally the free world.

Out of the seven members of my family, I was the only one who couldn't stand the taste of root beer, or any other cola for that matter. So when my folk's would hit the A&W for food to go, they would buy a glass gallon jug of root beer for the rest of the clan (6), and a quart container of orange for me (1). Now I was never the smartest kid on the block, but I had a good grasp of basic division of fluid ounces. I can safely say that this was one of the few times that I came out on top.

I can't remember whether it was because of a challenge, or just some intense flirting with one of the car-hops, but my brother Doug had been on a mission to eat/drink one hundred root beer floats over the course of one summer. I don't know where they kept track of this data of his float consumption, but sometime near summer's end, Doug was crowned Root Beer Float King. He was presented with his own giant A&W Root Beer mug. Doug's name, title, and achievement were marked upon it.

As the years went by, I progressed from the back of the bus, to the front. I had also progressed from hoping the carhops roller-skates would hang up on a wad of gum, to hoping those same skates would hang around my car, and linger just a little longer.

Eventually I came to recognize what a great social gathering place these drive-ins were. It didn't matter whether you were driving a sports car, a pick-up, or a motor-cycle, you were all there for basically the same reason and it definitely wasn't because of the food.

I can only wonder, where those carefree days, the cute carhops, and that big heavy mug went to.

OF MICE AND BOYS

My very first recollection of mice occurred when I was four years old. The whole family was sitting around the dinner table when we heard a **snap,** come from the other room. My dad's eyes lit up as he shouted "*AH-HAH!*" and left the table. About a minute later we heard the toilet flush. My dad came back to the dinner table with a victorious look on his face. We asked what happened. "*Got a mouse in the old mouse trap*" he replied. Having heard the snap of the trap, and then the toilet flush, Dan (who was three at the time) asked dad if the mouse had needed to go to the bathroom. Dad smiled and said "Yep!"

About a year later we had moved out into the country and soon to follow Dan became the proud owner of a white mouse. I can't remember where this mouse came from but he kept it in a glass gallon jar. I think he called it <u>Whitey</u>. Dan loved this mouse as much as any boy ever loved any dog. Unfortunately there came a morning when Dan woke up early and discovered that his mouse had escaped it's glass jar and was indeed missing. Dan ran frantically through the house waking and inlisting everybody in his search. I remember hearing the commotion and sitting up in my bed at about the exact moment that Dan's search party entered my room. There was a scream, and then someone pointed to my bed. And then I screamed.

The pieces of the puzzle finally fell into place. During the night, the mouse had escaped his jar, and somehow wound up in my bed, where during my sleep, I must have rolled over on it and suffocated it with my little five year old body. I can't remember whether we buried it in the back pasture or gave it a burial at sea in the bathroom. The back pasture was traditionally saved for larger animals, so I'm betting on the bathroom. I do remember however that Dan's attacks on me accelerated from that point on.

Many summers later found most of us kids changing irrigation pipe for the local farmers. Changing irrigation pipe is a little more complicated than it first sounds. Piece by piece you have to pick up the twenty foot pipe that is half full of water and carry it forty feet to the next outlet. If the sprinkler risers are fairly tall they become top heavy and are prone to tipping over. Consequently you have to lay the pipe while there is water running through it from the main line. When there is water running through the pipe you have to make your connection quickly and accurately or your stuck holding a twenty foot- 4" in diameter pipe full of water. If you're slow, the pipe fills up while your holding it and quickly exceeds your own body weight. This happens very fast when your only ninety pounds of p_ss and vinegar.

The prevailing wage for a day of this work was a dollar an hour. I don't think there was any retirement plan and there were only a few benefits. One of which was that you could eat all the raw corn you wanted, which is mighty refreshing on a hot day, but unfortunately only is available during a short time each summer. The other benefit came from the actual work. When you find yourself carrying a twenty foot- 4" pipe that is half full of water, you can do weight lifting curls while you walk, which is great for the arms and stomach. Picking up a twenty foot-4" pipe half full of water, also does wonders for your balance, as you have to pick it up in the middle and hope that the water comes out equally at both ends, or you run aground.

The other strange benefit to this type of work was in the laying of the pipe. As I said before, you have to align this pipe while there is water running through it. Traditionally you change pipe in rubber boots, tenny-runners, or bare feet. Now on a hot boring day, and you are laying hundreds of pieces pipe, and you happen to notice a field mouse hole near the end of the pipe, I defy anyone **NOT** to divert the water into that hole.

Anytime you divert this much water into a mouse hole, eventually the little buggers come out. At this point you do what can only be described as a twisted version of the "*Boot Scoot Boogie.*" As the water pours into the hole and the mice pour out of the ground, you tend to work yourself into a stomping frenzy. When you are barefoot it is always best to use your heel as it is the most callused and has no conscience of it's own.

I was in the midst of one of these stomps one day when I noticed something dark out of the corner of my right eye. Thank god **it** had approached from the right, because **<u>Death</u>** usually approaches from the left. Anyway, about an arms length away from my right foot was a rat about the size of a really big tennis shoe. He was just standing there with his arms crossed, tapping his foot on the ground. Swear to god, he was tapping his foot on the ground. He looked at the mice massacre, and than at my foot, and then again at the mice massacre, and once again at my foot. At this point in history Bob Beamon held the world long jump record at about 29 feet. I shattered that by a good three feet but alas there were no witnesses.

On occasion we would employ weapons for the demise of the rodent populace. We'd go out to the hay shed and turn bales over, which would reveal nests. When the little fellas started scootin, we started shootin. I was using a 22 rifle. Dan, not to be out-gunned, was using his semi-automatic deer rifle. Now given the fact that his shells were

74

larger than the average mouse, I can safely say that more of the mice died of heart failure, than gunshot wounds. It was actually kind of a disturbing scene. All those cute little mice clutching their chests and then just falling over. I hope writing about this doesn't bring back the nightmares. I was doing so well for so long.

I worked with a guy a few years back who used to catch mice, tape them to an arrow, and then fire them straight up into the air. As a kid, I'd seen hundreds of westerns, I had arrows, I had tape, I had mice, why the heck hadn't I thought of this?

So many mice, so little time.

IN SEARCH OF

My parents were very efficient and organized people. There is no doubt in my mind that both would have achieved greatness, if their five untamed offspring hadn't broken their will to live. While other parents were in search of bigger houses and newer cars, mine were in search of all items that we kids had lost, and a much-deserved rest.

Of the many items we kids lost, we generally lost tools. Many people collect tools so that they can say they have them. They don't necessarily need them, and most often don't even use them. Tools represent an image. Case in point; The weekend carpenter who buy's $300 worth of tools to build a $17 birdhouse, video tapes the entire project, and can't seem to get a bird to go near it.

My dad had more tools than any one I knew. He worked as a diesel mechanic, welder, carpenter, machinist, electrician, millwright, etc. He wore out more tools than most people would ever hope to own. When you are a millwright, you have to keep the sawmill running. This means you have to have the ability, knowledge, and tools to fix everything in that sawmill. From buzz saws, gang saws, massive conveyor systems, peelers, to Hawgs that can turn log ends, to shreds in about a second and a half. A mill is a paradox in the aspect that it is both living and dying at the same time. It is very difficult to keep these giants in operation, as they run twenty-four hours a day, seven days a week. My dad kept these giants on their feet for many years, and now my brother Jim does. It requires an extraordinary amount of intelligence, backbreaking work, little sleep, and lot's and lot's of tools.

The old man had a number of huge wooden chests that

were full of every tool imaginable, and the walls of his tool shed were lined with even more. If you could fit all of the old mans tools into a 3/4 ton pick-up (which you couldn't) the truck would've been too heavily laden to move. By the time the last one of us kids moved out of the house however, all he had left was an old claw hammer (with only one claw) a monkey wrench, and a bunch of empty tool chests. All other tools, we kids had managed to lose, or accidentally destroy.

The old man was always building things, and our mom was always right beside him. I often wondered whether this was because of her love of building things with her husband or her fear of being alone with the fearsome five. It must've been her love of building and her love for her husband, because she kept on building things with him long after the kids were gone.

Sometimes in the middle of a project, one of them would come up to one of us kids, and before they could even speak, the kid would say "*What coping saw?*" Now this wasn't some sort of ESP on our part. We had just lost so many of his tools that eventually we had acquired this prophetic ability to not only know which one we'd lost most recently, but which one he'd most likely need next. It was always amazing to my dad that while his kids had this gift of knowing what they'd lost, they hadn't a clue as to even which county they might have lost it in. What can I say, we were indeed, gifted.

Growing up with a builder, all of us kids naturally spent a great deal of time doing the same. We would help him with all projects great and small. Employing us kid's as his assistants only resulted in it taking him about three times as long to get the work done, but he didn't seem to mind. It takes an extraordinary amount of patience to build something with the help of five spastic assistants.

While he was at work, we'd tackle our own projects with some of his knowledge, a lot of sweat, and all of his tools. The big difference was that when the old man built a boat, it floated, and ours sank. His buildings stood tall and proud, while ours leaned and usually fell over. He'd use a tenth of the lumber and nails that we would, but he would have something to show for it. We not only wouldn't have much to show for it, but it got to the point that we would lose tools we weren't even using. Figure that one out if you can, my dad never could.

Part of the problem was basic tool abuse. We would use wrenches for hammers, hammers for pick-axes, pick-axes for weapons, weapons for tools, I think you get the picture. There is even a vague recollection of using a rifle to shoot a much-needed hole through a piece of wood one time. God knows where the drill was, or what we were building, but as always, the important thing was to get the task at hand done. And we always did. Sometimes. Kinda. Sorta.

Many years later found me living in the mountains and the proud father of a small boy, who was born in the spring. My folks drove seven hundred miles to come see their grandson. The following Christmas my dad sent me two brand new screwdrivers. The following summer I was on a wood cutting expedition with just my boy and myself. He was a little over a year old then and I was still training him on not being frightened of the chain saw. By the looks of his diaper I was failing miserably.

I would park him near where I was cutting, fire up the chain-saw, and then make faces at him while I cut the logs. Eventually he became fairly relaxed around the noise, allowing me to continue cutting. At some point during my cutting he commenced to get into the milk crate I kept my gas, bar-oil, and tools in, and proceeded to lose one of my Christmas screwdrivers into the forest. I needed the one he lost to keep the chain saw running properly. I have never been able to figure out how a fourteen-month-old baby, sitting in one spot of the forest floor, could make a tool completely vanish. I looked and looked for that screwdriver but never could find it. Karma perhaps? You be the judge, I already know the verdict.

A half dozen years after my dad died, I was digging through some boxes of my childhood stuff, which were stored in his attic. In one of the boxes, I ran across a little screwdriver that I could remember him buying some thirty years earlier. He only used it for a month or two before it was also lost. It was a clever little thing that had a sliding claw apparatus that when slid forward, opened and then closed around the head of the screw, holding it onto the screwdriver tip. It was just great for fixing things in tight spots that could only be reached by one hand. How it got into that box is as big a mystery as what happened to the rest of his tools, and apparently now mine.

BOYS-R-US

I haven't completely figured out why boys were invented, nor have I totally figured out their purpose. OK, having sired three boys of my own, I have a pretty good grasp of the *perpetuation of the species* theory. You don't get to be forty without a basic understanding of where the little critters come from, and how they got there. I was raised in the country where there was perpetuating going on all over the place for God sake. What I <u>don't</u> understand is why boys think and act the way they do. I used to be, and at times still am one, and I still can't figure em out.

They have neither rhyme nor reason for their behavior. They are blessed with a simple view of everything in the world which is to be admired in this day and age, but it still makes one scratch one's head at their actions. They excel at destruction and general mayhem. They are without a doubt the most disgusting, vile creatures that ever half learned to eat. They will put anything in their mouths, except of course something of nutritious value.

They neither look at a glass of milk as half-full or half-empty, they tend to view it as something to either spill or to break. When they spill it they merely say "*oopsie*". When they break it, they hide the pieces in the flour bin or in your shoes. That way, in their own mind, you will never find it, and they really believe this to be true. And when you cut your foot open while putting on your shoes, there is the damnedest look of consternation on their faces, because they really are surprised at the chain of events that just took place. And then the really strange thing happens. They just move on. They move forward as if nothing has just taken place.

Boys also have a penchant for causing great pain on small creatures. It's instinctive and I'm starting to question whether or not they ever outgrow it. I knew a kid in school who dug somewhere into his twisted mind and came up with the idea of having his own pet fly. He had managed to pull a long strand of hair from a girl classmate, tie it into a slipknot, and place the loop around the head of a fly. At this point in the game, he literally had a fly, on a leash, as a pet. He would show everybody his pet fly and the trick it would do. The fly would sit in his left hand until he would say "_fly_" and then he would raise his right hand which had the other end of the hair attached to it. This would jerk the fly up into the air where it felt compelled to fly in circles. Most people couldn't see the strand of hair he was using for a tether. They were fairly impressed until he jerked a little too hard one time, and popped the fly's head off. Bummer. Last I heard he was selling macramé somewhere. Double bummer.

My brother Doug spent some time one summer building houses in Arkansas. He fell into a band of local bare-footers who showed him how to stick a piece of straw up the keester of a firefly, causing it to fly straight up into the atmosphere, and then straight back down to earth to it's death. Cool. Amongst that group and most other groups of kids, there was always some ballyhoo about the concept of turning a grasshopper's head halfway around, causing it to jump backwards. I can't tell you if this works as all my attempts failed miserably. *Oopsie*.

At a fairly early age I discovered that holding a snake by the tail and playing crack the whip is the only safe, sure-fire way to make a snakes tongue longer. It is also a very effective way to get rid of that pesky coiling action that snakes are prone to. Of course the down side to this is that without their ability to slither and coil, they just sort of lay there in a straight line until they eventually fall over. It's a subtle fall, that kind of resembles a roll, but nonetheless, technically it is a fall.

One of my mom's brothers learned a neat trick with chickens. He discovered this about sixty years ago and passed it on to me as a kid. You draw a large circle in the dirt with your finger, about three feet in diameter or larger. You then grab a chicken by its legs and spin him around your head. I can't remember the exact amount but I'm guessing that a dozen laps ought to do it. You then place the chicken in the middle of the circle. If it just lies there, then it's probably dead and you have a pretty good idea what's for supper. You also may want to cut down on the amount of laps of the next volunteer. If the chicken survives, then it will wander around like a drunken sailor, but it will not leave the circle. Even in its dizzy frame of mind, it recognizes the line in the dirt as a snake trail, and will turn around and head the other way.

Now I haven't a clue as to how a small boy stumbles onto this kind of scientific information. Was he just laying in bed one day when it dawned on him to draw a ring on the ground and throw a dizzy chicken in the middle? I don't know why boys are cursed with abnormal thought patterns, but I do know that there are few things as funny looking as a well spun chicken, or as tasty as an over-spun one.

O.S.H.A.

It is always tragic when someone gets hurt, on or off the job. The pain and suffering is tremendous, but sometimes not nearly as painful as when you have to explain how the accident occurred.

A long time ago, while employed as a private carpenter to the owners of a sawmill, I had to fill out my first accident report. I had acquired my injury on the job so consequently in that little tiny space on the form, I had to recount the horror of what took place the previous afternoon. I was building fence on that unforgettable day, when another guy and myself decided to take a break. I had sat down and had just taken a bite of my bologna sandwich, when I realized that I had sat down on a roll of barbed wire, thus puncturing my right butt. Since it was rusty, (the wire) the foreman insisted I go get a tetanus shot. The **R.O.B.W.I.** (Roll Of Barbed Wire Incident) was responsible for the round scar on my butt. The "V" shaped scar right next to it was the result of an **E.W.K.I** (Errant Woodcarving Knife Incident) some dozen years earlier, but I'd rather not go into that right now.

Dr. Drost, the same doctor that brought me into this world for $75.00, gave me the tetanus shot. During this office visit he told me the story of a patient of his that had also worked at the sawmill. This man pulled green chain and had a habit of leaving when the big boards came down the line. His excuse was that he had to go to the outhouse. He would then linger in the outhouse until the heavy boards were finished. This habit greatly upset the rest of the men on the green chain. Realizing that they had no right to deprive a man of a trip to the outhouse, their only retaliation was to make his visit as uncomfortable as possible. So they hid the toilet paper.

Having grown up in the country, I knew what the doctor was about to tell me before he even said it. I knew from much experience, that when you find yourself in the great outdoors without toilet paper, you have two choices. You can use leaves (which contrary too popular belief, does not get the job done and is generally not present in a sawmill outhouse anyway) or you simply cut off part of the flannel shirt that your wearing. First goes the tails then go the pockets. It is critical at this point that you remove all buttons. Having done laundry for one husband, one tomboy daughter and four sons, my mom can testify to the deteriorated condition of all of our flannel shirts. Our shirts just kept getting shorter until eventually there would be nothing left but a collar. Kind of makes you wonder about those Chippendale dancers doesn't it? Well of course it doesn't.

Anyway, back to the guy in the outhouse. Realizing his desperate need for toilet paper, he went about his business just like we use to. He grabbed a shirt tail, pulled out his pocketknife, and started cutting upwards. The problem came when the seam of his shirt, put up a little fight, and he jerked up so hard, that the knife cut threw the seam, kept going north, and damn near remove his nose from his face. Dr. Drost sewed his nose back on and advised him not to catch a cold for a while.

My brother Jim told me a story about a coworker at his mill. The guy was walking by a piece of machinery that had an opening about the size of a finger. Without thinking, the guy stuck his finger into the hole and promptly ground off the tip of it. Naturally, he started jumping up and down and screaming. When his coworkers ran over, they saw all the blood and asked him what happened. The guy told them "*I just stuck my finger in that hole, like this*" And I'll be damned if he didn't grind off some more.

My brother Doug was working in Bayhorse, Idaho about a dozen years ago. He and his crew were taking core samples out of the mountain, when a fellow worker somehow cut off two fingers. The geologist drove him to the hospital. While shutting down the equipment, Doug found the guy's fingers. He grabbed them and flew down the mountain in hot pursuit but got to the hospital fifteen minutes late. The doctor was just finishing sewing up the stubs. Realizing he was still carrying the digits in his hand, Doug asked the man if he wanted to keep them for a souvenir. The doctor missed a stitch, and the tough old fart almost decked Doug. I don't know what they did with the man's digits, but he was back on the job the next day.

Ten years later, Doug found himself running a crew of idiots in a remote Eskimo village. At this point I need to make it clear that the idiots mentioned were not Eskimos, but were the product of the lower forty-eight (that's us). Doug was building a schoolhouse and the idiots were mostly getting in his way. One idiot in particular was screwing around with a pneumatic nail gun one day and nailed his foot to the floor. The head of the nail was buried in the top of his boot, while the rest of the nail went all the way through his foot and into the floor. Doug had to slide a pair of wire-cutters between the bottom of the guy's boot and the floor to work at cutting him loose. He managed to cut the nail in two, effectively removing the idiot's foot from the floor. They then flew him the several hours to Anchorage to have the nail removed from his foot. Idiot or not, he was back on the job a few days later.

As long as we are on the subject of idiots, I know two

highly trained professional meat-cutters, named Steve and Dave. During a visit from the state health inspector, these two idiots were busy cleaning what the inspector felt was dirty. Steve was cleaning the meatslicer and Dave was scrubbing something in the sink, to the right of the meatslicer. Steve took a six-inch boning knife, turned on the meatslicer, and holding the knife very firmly, started shaving residue off the spinning twelve-inch slicer blade. Dave was four feet away at the sink when he heard a **KERPOW!** And noticed something flying past his nose. He looked over at Steve, who was still standing at the slicer, counting and inspecting his fingers, over and over again.

The single greatest contribution to the meat industry by **O.S.H.A**. in the last twenty years, was when they made the smock industry move the chest pocket from the outside of the smock, to the inside. It was **O.S.H.A.'s** thinking that when a meat-cutter bent over, he was less apt to have a pen or pencil fall out of their pocket thus preventing that meat-cutter from slipping on it at a later time and plummeting to his death. I have wrestled with **O.S.H.A**. and their idea's for twenty-five years and tend to feel that they are in the ***breasts on a boar*** category.

Now back to the two idiots in the meat department. While Steve was holding the knife against the spinning blade, the tip of the knife hit something and blew the knife out of his hand. Six inches of sharp blade went through his fingers yet didn't cut one. It also flew by Dave's face instead of into the side of his head. Once they were certain no harm was done, the two idiots bent over laughing hysterically and thanks to **O.S.H.A**. not one pen fell out of their pockets, hence, no needless deaths.

So if you ever wonder about the importance of self-indulgent government agencies trying to protect us from ourselves, just remember **Odd Sh_t Happens Anyway!**

SUNDANCE

I had spent a couple of years after high school working a variety of jobs and riding my thumb around America. One of the many jobs was working at the mill. Since millwork was both brutal and boring, and my travels had taken me almost fourteen thousand miles through thirty states, I was at a point where I needed a summer of honest work and a lot of swimming. So I went back to farming. I also needed a companion, so I went to the pound and bought a dog. This was during a simple time in my life when I knew I had adequate time to train him. The secret to successfully training a dog is to spend twenty-four hours a day, seven days a week with him. You simultaneously train the dog, while he trains you.

Mine was a mix of Husky and McNab Shepherd. He had small feet, a thick coat, and would grow to tip the scales at just under forty pounds. He was the perfect size for the road. He wound up with two names. He answered to both Sundance and Dancer.

Where ever I went so did Sundance. He would ride on my tractor or run beside it. While I drove truck, he rode shotgun. The bulldozer was the only piece of equipment that he steered clear of. I think it was the ground vibrating that bothered him. Since I was running a lot of noisy equipment, I decided to train him with hand signals. Because of this he never let his eyes off of me. We had many long talks with our eyes alone. I understood him, and he understood me.

A few years down the trail at our annual Mckenzie River White Water Run, we were crossing a highway with two blind corners. For some unknown reason when I ran across the highway, Sundance didn't immediately follow. I turned around and saw him just starting to cross the road at the same time that a loaded log truck rounded the corner, heading straight for him. I hand signaled him to stop, which he did, and the truck blew right past, missing him by no more than a foot or two. The only time he wasn't looking at me was as the truck went past, kicking up a lot of wind and dust. I can still see him sitting there with his eyes closed, ears flapping in the breeze.

I had also trained him to sit outside any building I entered and wait un-tethered until my return. Sometimes I would enter through one door, exit through another, and sneak around the corner and watch him. He would usually stand for the first five minutes, sit for the next five, and then look for a cool shady place to lay down and continue his vigil. On occasion I would give him a whistle from where I was hiding and watching. He would jump up, look to the door, then to the direction of the whistle, then to the door and then he would start dancing around and yipping not sure of what to do next. He knew he wasn't suppose to leave his post, but he also knew I had somehow whistled from outside.

I could put a piece of meat in his mouth and he would hold it in his teeth until I told him it was OK to eat it. I did this once and the phone rang. I went in and answered it and forgot about Sundance. About fifteen minutes later I remembered and went outside to discover that he'd gotten tired of this game and spit the meat out onto the ground and was just staring at it. I gave him the nod and he picked it back up and sucked it down.

Years later I was working at a lake resort in Nebraska. I did maintenance during the day and was the bartender at night. Sundance had full run of the grounds (as did I) and met many friends (as did I). The locals recognized his love of hitchhiking and would sometimes take him with them wherever they were going. Sometimes they'd tell me, sometimes not. They might drive up to me and say "*Me and Dancer are heading into Omaha for some parts, do you need anything?*" Or " *Me and Dancer just got back from Lincoln, I got him a cheeseburger and a Coke.*" I watched him leave one morning with a blonde in a Camaro, and return that afternoon with a guy in a dump truck. He caught rides on the back of the bush-hawg that we mowed the grounds with and even got to take a couple of spins on a Jet Ski. Like myself, he did love to travel.

One night I was closing down the restaurant/lounge along with five waitresses. We finished all the dishes, cleaned all the tables and had just started cutting the steaks for the next day. Someone said it was time to divvy up the tips, so we left the steaks on the table and went into the lounge where I fixed every one a drink. We were discussing that night's business and enjoying the free drinks when one waitress burst into the lounge screaming that there was a dog in the kitchen. I told her not to panic, that he was mine and just waiting for me to get off work. She was worried that he would eat the sixty pounds of steaks lying on the table. I told her to tell him not to. She did, and so he didn't. When we finished the business at hand and eventually made it back into the kitchen, Dancer was just laying under the table that held the still untouched steaks.

Several years later found me working at a Safeway in the Sierra Nevada's. I worked nights and took Sundance with me. He would sleep on the automatic doormat in the front of the store. The store opened one hour before my shift ended each day, and as the store manager would unlock the doors, he would also have to ask Sundance to move off of the doormat. He needed Dancer to move so as not to keep the automatic door open, and to also allow the customers to come inside. He not only moved, but over a period of time he didn't need to be asked.

He would sometimes disappear during my night shift and it took me several months to figure out where he would go. I would never have figured out where he went if one of the drivers hadn't come up to me one night and asked if the black dog was mine. He then went on to tell me that my dog knew the difference between a Safeway truck and all others. Apparently Sundance ignored all the other trucks that drove by each night, but whenever a Safeway truck would drive by he would circle the building, winding up at the back of the store. As the truck was backing into the unloading dock, Sundance would be waiting for the driver at the back door. The truck driver would then unlock the door, go into the meat cooler, dig a big bone out of one of the bone barrels and toss it to Dancer. This went on for many months before I ever caught wind of it.

Dancer and I went on many adventures together. He was with me when I was refused entrance into Canada, and was at my side several years later, when we eventually made it across. We got to see the Northern Lights and our first moose together. We panned for gold in the Sierra's, farmed in Oregon, melted from the heat in Las Vegas and crossed the continental divide about a dozen times. We weathered tornado's and killer hangovers in Nebraska, and froze our butt's off in Alaska. We even attended a union strike vote meeting together. I didn't ask how he voted and he didn't ask me, although we both had our suspicions. He watched me grow from a kid with an itchy thumb, to a parent with a floor full of twitchy critters.

A few months after I put Sundance to rest, I ran across his collar. I hesitated, but finally picked it up. I could still smell him. A World War Two pilot once told me that love comes and goes, but a man only gets one good dog in his life. I've been in love a number of times, and I've had a lot of dogs. The older I get, the less I know, but the more I understand. My friend the pilot was right. To the one good dog of my life.

Vio Con Dios old friend.

A PENNY AND MY THOUGHTS

If you take fifty pennies from 1954 and stack them next to the same amount from 1995 you will notice three things. The first and most apparent is that the new pennies are much shinier. The second is that the old stack is somewhat shorter. The third thing you notice is that you might be three pickles short of a barrel if you find yourself comparing stacks of pennies in the first place. Maybe this boy should get out more.

During World War Two the penny was made from recycled shell casings. In 1943, due to copper shortages, they were made of steel. Legend has it that twelve pennies were accidentally minted out of copper in that same year. Rumor further has it that only eleven of those have been accounted for. The twelfth would fetch a princely sum. It was always my dream to find that one.

The Navajo use to adorn their clothing with pennies and other coin. It was a sign of good fortune, which is ironic since in the big picture, we corralled them onto a reservation and pennies, is about all they received for what we took from them. My folks lived on a Navajo reservation, and my mom still has some of the Indian Head pennies, with holes bored through them so they could sew them on their clothing. To the average collector they are worthless because of the holes. To me they are priceless because of the stories they tell.

My brother Doug use to pound pennies down to make buttons for clothing and conchos for moccasins. He also flattened copper wire to decorate his leatherwork. The combination of copper and buckskin is a natural and very pleasing to the eye. My brother was quite good at his craft and I hope he takes it up again someday. I have a few pieces of his work and my greedy side would like a few more.

When I was a kid I used to take my summer's crop-pickin money, go to the bank, and buy two to three bags of pennies. Each bag contained 5,000 pennies, which I would dump out onto my bed and then separate the old wheatbacks from the newer Lincoln Memorials. Once I had completed this sorting process, I would return the newer pennies back to the bank. A teller would take the pennies and myself into the back room and dump them into a machine. This magnificent machine would make a lot of whirring and clanging noises as it counted the coins. When it was done counting, I would give the teller the difference required to buy yet another bag. I would then go home and start this routine over. The first summer I did this, I figured out that each bag averaged about 9% wheatbacks. Several years later when I quit this method of collecting, it was down to 2%.

Later, as a teenager, I chose to sell them for an automobile repair debt I had accrued with the **Bank of DAD**. He didn't make me, nor wanted me to sell my coin collection, but I didn't want to be in debt. So there the two bulls stood. One older and wiser, one younger and just entering the world of responsibility. Without their having verbally told me, my parents had instilled in me the distaste of debt. My mom told me a quarter of a century later, that she would sooner pick sh_t with the chickens, than be beholden to someone else. I am eternally grateful to have had them as parents and as friends.

There were too many pennies to count, so I figured out how many were in a pound, and then weighed them on a scale. I sold roughly forty pounds of the old pennies for about a hundred and twenty dollars. If memory serves me, it worked out to just under three cents apiece. I had also acquired a fairly healthy collection of silver coins, which I also sold. I had nominal regrets then and absolutely none now. As it turns out, I would also rather pick sh_t with the chickens, then be in debt.

In the seventies this nation experienced a lot of shortages and an inflationary monster that hadn't been seen in quite a while. I watched gas go from twenty-five cents a gallon to forty-cents in a heartbeat. I had to get in line three to four hours before the pumps opened just to have a chance of getting gas. The gas stations would open at 8:00 a.m. and be out of gas before noon. While waiting in these lines the main talk among the people was that if gas ever hit fifty cents a gallon, *BY GOD WE WILL WALK!* Well it did and we didn't. During this same time, copper prices also went through the roof. It was approaching a point where it was about to cost more then a penny to make a penny.

While copper was fetching such good prices, my kid brother and I had been working in and out of the sawmill. During our travels we had noticed a large hunk of electrical wire in the mills refuse yard. The only moral thing to do would be to ask the owners if we could have it, but since we had a pretty good idea what their answer would be, we decided to resort to twilight appropriating. Our plan was to park Dan's old Willys pick-up quite away from the yard, sneak in, grab the wire and run.

The first problem we faced was that this hunk of wire was about four inches in diameter and I can't remember how long. It outweighed both of us and took quite a bit of work to drag it all the way back to his pick-up. The second problem was wrestling this dead electric eel up into his pick-up and the third was what to with it once we had it.

We opted to drive a dozen miles of country back roads to our folk's house and hide it in the old man's tool shed. Sometime during the next few days, we started hearing on the local news that copper prices had gotten so high that people were actually stealing it and selling it to salvage yards. They also said that the salvage yards were contacting the police when they suspected any wire was stolen. My folks commented on what a crazy time we were living in. They were use to Dan and myself sweating on a regular basis, so they didn't comment on our current nervous condition.

Dan and I had a couple a hundred pound monster in the old man's tool shed that we now didn't know what to do with. We did know however that we had better do something before the old man discovered it. The only thing we could do was to start cutting this thing into little pieces and unraveling it to make it look less like it's former self. We then took it to the one salvage man in town that could be trusted. His name was Willy. Being that we are now in the nineties, I can't print the last part of his nickname. This was a long time ago, and things were different back then. Right or wrong, Willy also referred to himself as Willy the ____. Nobody was politically correct in the seventies, including Willy.

Anyway, Willy gave us fair market price, a funny look, and that was the last time we pulled a stunt like that. Well anyway that was the last time we pulled a stunt identical to that. We were young and stupid and frankly, pretty damned good at it. I like to think that the copper we appropriated went on to become pennies. I know it didn't, but it's nice to think it did. Willy did point out however that he could have given us twice as much per pound if we hadn't cut it into all those little pieces. Apparently in it's original length it was of a high enough quality to make jumper cables and all sorts of other things.

I started over with my collecting and twenty-five years later, I have again amassed about twenty-five pounds of the old wheatbacks. I've collected this second batch without buying bags. I'll be honest with you, I don't know where they all came from, but the bag keeps getting heavier.

There is talk again in Congress, about discontinuing the minting of my beloved penny. This comes up every half dozen years or so and I always get a sad feeling when they consider it. The Lincoln penny has been around since 1909 and has become the most enduring coin minted since America's beginning. It's only major change came in 1959 when they switched the back from wheat stalks to the Lincoln Memorial. If you look closely you can see Abe in the middle of the memorial. He was always my favorite president.

Like myself, many of the older pennies have lost their luster, but not their purpose. Sure, they don't go as far as they used to, but then again, neither do I. Pennies have been spent, dropped, rolled, thrown, beaten, flipped, buried, scratched, burned, pinched, lost and even intentionally discarded, to lay there for long periods of time before someone else picks them back up. Sounds familiar, although I've never been tossed into a fountain for good luck. Yet.

The reason they don't stack as high as the newer ones is because over the years all of their activity has worn them down to a thinner version of themselves. Again, a familiar sound. I've only been around about half as long as the Lincoln penny and the only thinning I've done is at the hairline, certainly not the waistline. Although I still have an old growth at the timberline, but since that's probably in poor taste and has nothing to do with pennies, I have to apologize for bringing it up. On second thought; no I don't. HeeHee.

SPORTS

Growing up in the country was a very physical experience. There was an overabundance of hard work that needed doing at all times and my folks had a very simple rule: work hard and play hard. Our folk's philosophy and our natural surroundings made for very athletic young boys, so consequently we played all sports.

Since we had to make do with what was available to us, we would high jump and pole vault into a sawdust pile out by the round corral. We did this until the track world switched from the Western roll to the Fosbury flop. Because of the new heights the rest of the world (and us boys) were achieving with the flop, and the fact that the flop makes you land on your neck and shoulders, we realized we needed something softer to land on.

It was a ritual of spring that as soon as the rain slowed down, and the weather warmed up, we would abandon our beds and sleep in the back yard. Since we didn't use our mattresses all summer, we agreed that they would make the perfect high jump pit. We had a long bamboo pole (that we had salvaged from a carpet store in town) which we would put between two of the old man's saddletree's. To advance the height we would use encyclopedias and any other books lying around.

My folks would get home from a hard day at work, walk in the front door, notice all the encyclopedias missing and say to each other how great it was that they had produced such good kids with a keen interest in reading. They would then notice that there wasn't a mattress or a couch cushion to be found in the house and all hell would subsequently bust loose. If I remember correctly, our world high jump record was one saddletree, nine encyclopedias, a Sears Roebuck catalog and three Readers Digests.

We each sought our own records at whatever we were doing. Brother Jim held the high school record by doing somewhere between 50 and 53 push-ups in thirty seconds. He then set his sights on the school bardip record. To do a bardip you need two posts about chest high and a little more than shoulder width apart. You then support yourself with one hand on each post, lower yourself until your hands are practically into your armpits, and then push yourself back up. This was one of the toughest records in high school. Jim went and planted a post parallel to a fence-post out by the chicken shed and practiced nightly until he could finally do a little over a hundred bardips at a time.

I had been eyeing Jim's high school push-up record and decided to attempt to beat it one day. We would do push-ups on a bench allowing you to not only to push up but to also pull down, thus letting you exceed the gravitational pull and save time. It was kind of a ***Type A*** push up. The coach held the stopwatch while one student put his hand on the bench where your chest had to hit to qualify for a push-up. As your chest would hit his hand, the student would yell out the count. While all this was going on, another student held your feet onto the bench to keep them from flying off. Believe it or not this really sometimes happens when you're hitting almost two push-ups per second. Well anyway, the coach said go, and I commenced doing push-ups like a damn Singer sewing machine. I was doing real well too until for some unknown reason at push-up # 43, I flew clean off the bench, dragging the guy holding my feet with me. We landed in a crumpled heap, with the bench lying on top of both of us. Jim's record was still safe. To this day, as close as I can figure, sweaty palms must've been the culprits.

As I was too little for football, and too short for basketball, I tried wrestling for a little while. I thought I was 73 pounds of spit and gristle and actually won my first couple of matches due to forfeits, since the other teams didn't have any gnomes in my weight category. Then one day found me at an away meet and across the mat was the meanest looking little pitbull of a wrestler I'd ever seen before. His beady little eyes were staring right through me and he was growling and salivating like a rabid wolf. I went over and asked my coach which poor s.o.b. had to wrestle the little pitbull. The coach put his forefinger on my chest. I looked again at my opponent. At that point, his growls were getting more intense, the saliva puddle was getting larger, and I was pretty sure I could see little flecks of foam forming around the corners of his mouth. I asked the coach what I had done to make this total stranger mad at me. The coach explained to me that the kid was trying to psyche me out. I told the coach it was working. The coach then told me to get back on the bench and try to out psyche him. So I sat down, stared right back, and gave my best shot at growling and salivating. Given a little more time I probably could've mustered up some foam of my own, but the referee pointed to us two growling Chihuahua's and onto the mat we went.

I really can't remember who won, which means I must have lost. I do know that he didn't pin me though. Just because your going down, doesn't mean you give up. I really didn't mind losing and to this day, I still don't, but I just will not stand for people foaming at the mouth and growling at me. Just ask my kids.

My brothers and I did our share of running also. *We ran through the briars and we ran through the brambles and we ran through the bushes where the rabbits wouldn't go, we ran so fast that the hounds couldn't catch us, on down the Mississippi to the Gulf of Mexico......* **Hey, wait a cotton pickin minute, just what the heck is going on here!** I'm trying to reminisce about my youth and all of a sudden, old songs from the War of 1812 are weaving in and out of my childhood memories. I've never been to the Gulf of Mexico. Anyway I don't think I have. That's the sort of thing you should remember isn't it? Maybe my mom is right, maybe over the years I have received one too many blows to the head. The brain never is quite the same after a few concussions. Anymore it just takes to wandering about where ever it wants to go.

Now where was I? Ah yes, I was running the 440 relay at a Confederate track meet and ~~~~ **Well dang, there it goes again.**

SISTERS

My dad had six brothers and four sisters. My mom had seven brothers and four sisters. I have three brothers and one sister. My boys each have two brothers and no sisters. Simple math tells you that sisters are evil and are in the slow process of being eliminated. Serves them right. Their first problem is that they are girls. There second is that they are not boys. I'm serious, they really aren't. Just look at em, they're built different and they act goofy.

My mom was the last of twelve kids born over a twenty-five year period. She then grew up to have five kids in six and a half years, proving once again to be the most efficient cuss I've ever met. I can only imagine the look she gave the old man when they left the hospital with gnome #5. My sister Linda was the firstborn and probably gave my folks the same look when they once again failed to bring home a sister and showed up with yet another brother.

One of my first recollections of my sister was also that of my first Halloween. She was dressed as an Indian princess and I was the papoose strapped on her back. I can't remember how many treats she got or whether or not she shared them with me, but I do remember that she removed me from her back a lot, complaining that I was too damn heavy. Since this was a full decade before Neil Diamond sang *"He ain't heavy, he's my brother"* I found myself walking a lot between house stops.

With both parents working a lot of hours trying to keep beans on the stove, Linda helped out by doing a lot of the cooking. Our mom is an excellent cook and Linda became one as well. The two of them also loved festivity and would take every opportunity to decorate either us or the house for whatever occasion they saw fit. Typical girl fashion, they did this with or without us boy's help or permission. They were not only girls, but they were also older than we boys, which left us in one hell of a predicament were. Periodically we would ask the old man for permission to exterminate them. He'd always say no, and we'd ask if it were because they were girls. He'd say it wasn't because they were girls, it was because they had seniority over us boys. Damn the unions.

One day, Linda decided to throw a fancy wedding anniversary dinner for our folks. She made us all clean and decorate the house (and ourselves) while she made a fancy meal. She put a bed-sheet on the dinner table, and covered it with flowers and candles. She then made my kid brother Dan and myself dress up like little barefoot waiters. We even had those silly towels draped over our left arm, which even to this day I don't understand. If I remember correctly, our job was to ask our parents if they wanted some more water with their dinner, which seemed pretty stupid since the sink was damn near within arms reach of where mom was sitting anyway.

Jim and Doug were also dressed up in silly attire and one of their job's was to slide mom and dad's chair under them when they sat down, (another totally unnecessary job in our eyes) and then serve the different courses of food that Linda had spent the day whipping together.

Linda turned the lights out, had one of us dumb waiters light the candles, and mom and dad commenced eating. With very few exceptions, I do not like shoveling unidentified food in my mouth without the benefit of light. I have no doubt that the two females at this shindig felt that the candlelight was romantic, but I'm also equally sure that the five males would have preferred a good old fashioned 100 watt bulb hanging over the food. It was instinct within the male populace at my house to want to not only sniff the food but to visually inspect it as well before eating it. This keeps you from accidentally eating a bug or other things you may not want to. This is a tried and true system.

Dad went along with eating in the dark until he bit into a chili teppin that Linda had used in one of the entrees. Now here's a little known fact, the U.S. Government denies this but it is indeed the truth. NASA regularly used chili teppins as rocket fuel until they worked the kinks out of liquid hydrogen. In the long run liquid hydrogen was much safer, but it never did give the same base thrust that the chili teppin provided, making it take a little longer to get the rocket off the ground and into space. Anyway, the chili teppin made my dad's blue eyes emit a red ray that blew the fork right out of my mom's hand. He then very convincingly said to turn on the damn lights. We did. The old man never minced words nor had to repeat sentences, that's just the way it was.

We four boys could tell by the look on his face that the old man was reconsidering the death versus seniority issue. My brothers and I wanted to applaud Linda for the fireworks we had just seen, and to tell her that we now considered her one of the boys. Linda however, was nowhere to be found. She was off somewhere crying. Boys cry when they get a whippin, girls cry without a whippin. I told you girls are goofy. Dad finished wrestling with the death versus seniority dilemma and Linda got to keep growing up with us four boys. I'm glad the old man let her stay. Sisters are goofy, but Linda's the kind you don't mind having for one.

NUTRIA

Nutria, or Coypu as they are known in South America, are a large rodent with webbed hind-legs and a long fur-less tail. They are indigenous to South America and parts of Canada. The other day I dug out my tattered old hitchhiking diary/atlas, and discovered that if you draw a line between South America and Canada, (now granted it's kind of a crooked line) bingo, roughly halfway between the two, is Alabama. And guess what? There is nutria in Alabama as well. I grew up 3000 miles to the west of Alabama, and this is where it gets real eerie. There is also a smattering of nutria around the farms in this state. Now how did a farm in Oregon get a species of animal, 3000 miles off of it's normal migratory pattern? Well, hold on to your knickers and I'll tell you.

If your way up in the air looking down on Alabama, and you head due east, what do you suppose you run into? That's right, Egypt. And what is Egypt famous for? That's right, Pyramids. And what do we know about pyramids? Right again, early space travelers. OK, a nutria's habitat is to live in swamp-like environments and live off of fresh water plants. Well I guess we all know how few swamps there are in Egypt. Well actually, I don't know how few swamps there are in Egypt, but I'm guessing not very many.

The nutria obviously needed a different place to live so they fled Egypt heading west to South America, Northern Canada, and Alabama via space ships. Now the way I see it, some poor space alien overshot his destination (by about 3100 miles) and crashed into the Pacific Ocean. There, the nutria abandoned their sinking spacecraft, swam to shore and that is precisely why we now have them in Oregon. If you think about it, this makes much more sense than them coming across the Oregon Trail in a string of those tiny, little connestoga wagons.

I saw my first nutria about three decades ago, at roughly age ten. I was down by the slough, when I spotted Charlie, (one of the farmers nine sons) carrying a gunnysack that seemed to have a life of it's own. I asked Charlie what he had in the bag, and he said he had found a twenty-pound rat in the cornfield. Having never heard of a rat of that size before, I was tempted to call him a liar, but as he was older and bigger than I was, I didn't. Judging however from the contortions the bag was going through, what ever it was he had in the sack, was big, wide-awake, and in a foul mood.

I carefully peeked into the sack and saw what appeared to be about a twenty-pound rat, only it had webbed back feet, and some pretty nasty looking yellow teeth. The most disturbing things about rodents are their nasty yellow teeth, it still gives me goose-bumps just thinking about them. Anyway, we went up to the big farm house, called the Fish and Wildlife department, and told them we had discovered a brand new species of some kind of giant duck-rat type creature. Fame and fortune we were sure was soon to follow.

The Fish and Wildlife department sent out a man with a big cage trap, who asked us to show him where we had spotted this duck-rat so that he could try to safely catch it. We told him that Charlie already had it stuffed into a gunnysack down by the slough. He started to ask how we'd gotten it into a gunnysack and then shook his head and said that he didn't want to know. He'd been out to the farm before and knew to expect, the unexpected. We took him down to the slough, where we dumped the critter out of the sack and into the cage.

The man then explained to us that the animal was a nutria, and that it had been used in the fur industry, as a replacement to the declining beaver populations back when everybody was wearing beaver hats. When the fashion industry quit making stove-pipe hats, there was less demand for the nutria so in a lot of areas the nutria farms just turned them loose, where they grew to become a nuisance to local crop farmers. Now just who did this man think he was talking to, a couple of dumb farm boy's? He didn't say a word about the pyramids, space aliens, or how the nutria got here from Alabama, and I think we all know what that means. That's right. Conspiracy!

From that day forward we all had a common goal, which was to eradicate the entire nutria population. The farmers gave us the green light, so we spent a lot of our leisure time hunting them (the nutria, not the farmers, although there were many times we were tempted.) My parents even supported us in our endeavor to the point that they would mount my kid brother and I (fully armed) to the front of their car, and we would drive the edges of the sloughs, shooting away at the nutria we'd turn up. Those were indeed good days.

Nutria live in burrows along the edges of swamps or slow moving creeks, and since we spent a lot of time fishing and swimming in those murky waters, we came into contact with them on a fairly regular basis. We didn't always have guns with us though, so we reached a comfortable truce with one another. This truce was of course broken if one of them got too close to you while you were swimming.

There are two things that make my skin crawl while I'm swimming, and that is either a snake or a twenty-pound rat swimming just a few feet away. At that point the gloves come off. Well actually you fly out of the water first, and then the gloves come off. Well no, actually most of the time we were skinny-dipping so there weren't any gloves to take off, but I think you know what I mean. As soon as nutria enters skinny-dipping water, it becomes an act of war.

During these skirmishes a rifle is the optimum weapon. If no rifle is present, rocks and big sticks are your next best choice. A baseball sized rock, or a bat sized stick being the most effective. You may think this a little severe, but I'm not talking about swatting flies here, I'm talking about clubbing nasty, yellow toothed rats that are the size of cocker spaniels. It's a good thing that we didn't have a lot of hikers or bird watchers happening by back then, as it might've been a little disturbing for them to see a small herd of naked muddy boy's flying out of a swamp, brandishing sticks and stones, and screaming like banshees.

One day a bunch of us were swimming and we came to a section of the creek that was chockfull of nutria trails and burrows. Now the one common denominator amongst all boys is their inability to stay out of caves. The laws of male youth are fairly rigid: If you see a cave, you have to go in it. It's as simple as that.

As we didn't have near enough caves around, a nutria den was the next best thing. So as it goes with boys, the next thing I know, I'm crawling naked into a nutria den. Now in all honesty, I was really hoping the den was empty, but in case it wasn't, I had with me one big damn stick. I was also dragging my little stick with me, but this is neither the time nor the place to get into that.

I was crawling on my belly, (Nutria dens do not have large openings) and pushing my stick (the big one) in front of me. I was also trying to adjust my eyes and ears to the darkness and the eerie silence. Three things happened at that point. **#1**, I could here breathing and a heartbeat, **#2**, my eyes had adjusted enough to see a dark mound in front of me, and **#3**, when I tapped that dark mound with my stick, I heard a very soft thud. Not a thud like I had hit it on the head or the back (*"Oh good, I knocked it out or paralyzed it"*), but more of an *"Oh my god I hit it on the belly, which is really gonna make it mad"* type thud.

When you are underground or in a cave there is virtually no light or sound other than that which you bring along. There is also no fear other than that which you bring with you. When I heard the thud of my stick, I immediately realized that a tapping is not a clubbing, and would only result in waking up the monster, not destroying it. There wasn't room to turn around (and I wasn't going to expose the hind end of my anatomy to those nasty yellow teeth anyway) nor was there time to crawl backwards out of the den. My only recourse was to start screaming and clubbing away as if my very life depended on it. After about an hour (actual elapsed kid time: 9 & 1/2 seconds) of primeval screaming and club flailing, the dust settled and I crawled backwards out of the den. There is a pretty good chance that I stuck my chest into the air and gave my own tiny rendition of Tarzan's victory scream, but I honestly don't remember.

After I calmed down a bit, and being that I was a normal bloodthirsty boy, I went and found some matches and crawled back into the nutria den to inspect the carnage. To both my dismay and relief, there was nothing in there. Apparently the heartbeat and the breathing I had been listening to, had been my own. What I had beat the hell out of was a mound of sand, which I could tell by match light had died almost instantly and painlessly.

When I came out of the den the other boy's asked me if I had killed it. I told them that it had died instantly and warned them not to go in there because it wasn't a very pretty sight. And it really wasn't.

BONES

One of the greatest flaws in the human anatomy is that of the bones. Now, don't get me wrong, the big guy upstairs did a pretty good job, it's just that he didn't consider the general problem of rambunctious boys. Their brains (and I use that term loosely) tend to push their activity level to the limit, and their bones seem to be the first casualty. If I could house one complaint with the big guy it would be of his mismatching the breaking strength of bones, with a boy's brain activity (or inactivity as the case may be.)

I broke my first arm (my left) at about four, and my second arm (my right) at around eight. Let me clarify for a moment here. I'm speaking in terms of years of age, not in terms of A.M./ P.M. And actually when I refer to breaking my first arm, I don't mean to imply that my left was the first arm I ever had. My memory has been muddied by too many concussions over the years, but I would bet that when I was born, it was a dead tie between my arms. Oh sure, I guess it's possible that the first thing Dr. Drost saw was my left hand coming out, snapping it's little fingers as if to say "*C'mon people, Let's kick it in high gear, I got places to go, people to see!*" But that's the sort of thing my mom would have mentioned by now. Then again, she's just diabolical enough, not to mention it at all. Hmmmm.....

Anyway, when I was four, I busted up my left arm badly enough that when the nurse met us at the emergency room door, she shouted "*Good Lord this boy has a compound fracture!*" and the next thing I know I'm on a gurney and there are two or three interns trying to hold me down (and barely succeeding) while another is sliding that horrible

Ether mask over my face. For a brief instant I was on a higher level of consciousness, birdies were singing and then everything went black.

I spent the next quite a few weeks in a cast, but for some reason, the bones healed so crooked that the doctor had to re-break my arm. I don't remember how he did it, nor really want to know. I do know that consequently I spent twice as long as normal wearing those darned casts. I was small enough, and the cast was big enough that I had to hold onto things in order to go up and down stairs, or I would occasionally tip over. Even on flat surfaces, sometimes all it took was a gust of wind or a well-aimed soccer ball to my head, to tip me over. My older brothers were as disappointed as I was relieved, when the cast finally came off for good.

When I turned eight, I broke my right arm, but by then wearing a cast was like shaking hands with an old friend. We had moved out into the country, and a cast just became a part of everyday life. I tried pounding a nail with it once, (that hurt) and tried using it for a baseball bat another time (that hurt like heck.) I could still do flips into grain bins, go fishing, ride bikes and horses, do chores etc. My mom even use to stick my arm inside plastic bread sacks and tape the dickens out of them, thus allowing me to go swimming with the rest of the clan. Our doctor was always amazed at the overall poor condition of my cast, and at the amount of grain and other items he would find in it when he'd cut it off. Eventually I went from a full cast (fingertips to armpit) to a half cast (fingertips to just below the elbow), allowing me even more mobility.

One day, all of us kids were helping my dad cut up a big oak behind our place. He'd cut, while we would load the wood into the truck. During a break from this work, Brother

Dan and I started throwing rocks into the slough. I was holding the rocks with my broken right arm, and throwing with my left. The funny thing about a cast, is that it is tight fitting in the beginning of it's career and very loose towards the end. When I got down to the last rock, I decided to fling it with my broken right arm. I threw the rock like you would a discus, and zingo, off flew the cast, as if in pursuit of the rock.

My pale arm just started rising up into the air, since it wasn't use to the lack of weight from the missing cast. Dan and I just stood there for a moment, spellbound by my arm mysteriously levitating, and then he told me I'd better get it back on before the old man found out. We owed a lot of money to the doctor at various times and I didn't even want to think how much a new cast would run. My folks never flinched at any of us going to the hospital, but they made it clear that you have to take care of what you have, and that included casts. Well my folks found out anyway, and they decided I didn't need to get a new one. This news made me very happy, as I finally had a cast I could take off on occasion. I could give my arm a bath once in a while, and instead of sticking a coat hangar down it to scratch an itch, or retrieve a penny, I could just pull it off. Life just couldn't get any better.

The only negative feelings I had about my second arm breaking were because of one bad doctor. I was screaming that the electric saw he was using to remove my full cast, was burning and cutting my arm. He kept saying that there was no way that the blade could be touching my arm, that I was just a scared little kid and that I should act like a man. Well he was wrong about the saw blade. It left a scar that runs from my wrist clear up halfway to my shoulder, to this very day. This was the second time that doctor had messed up while putting one of us seven back together, and it was also his last. My mom was a shy little redhead, but the hospital learned not to underestimate her.

All of us kids were cursed with short little chicken legs, and one day a man stopped my mom on the sidewalk and asked " *Do you know what's wrong with your five young-uns?*" My mom was very shy, but very protective of her herd, so this question kind of threw her for a loop. He then answered his own question by saying "*They were all born with their butt's to close to the ground*" and off he went laughing. My mom let him live and I'll never understand why.

Because of having those short legs, I've always been top heavy, and thus prone to tipping over, with or without a cast on my arm. In junior high I was recruited onto the track team because of my speed. Unfortunately I was restricted to the dashes because while I was incredibly fast in a straight line, during the longer runs I had a habit of falling over in the corners. More than once I'd ask how I did, just to be told "*Well, you had him beat going into the corner, and then, well, you know, you just sort of fell over!*"

In high school I purchased a pair of used skis, poles, boots and bindings, for ten bucks. On the top of the mountain, I crashed, and since my bindings didn't break free, my femur and fibula did. A broken leg has a little more restriction on your life than a broken arm, but you learn to adjust. Since I could no longer wear pants, my mom bought me a pair of farmer over-alls to wear to school. The other kids liked this look so much, that it became quite a fashion trend. Most of the other kids got theirs at Sears, Penny's, or Wards, with names like Big Mac, and Lee. My mom got mine from the feed store where she worked and I always chuckle over the irony of the brand name that started this trend. They were _Can't Bustems_, and they had a little yellow rooster embossed by the name.

Cabin fever sets in with restricting injuries and eventually I reached a point where enough was enough. I took my brother Doug's 500 Kawasaki on a couple of short joy rides, bearing in mind to go slow, and that if I did have to lay it down, to try to lay it down on the left side. I also borrowed his little convertible Sunbeam once. I worked the clutch, brake, and gas with my left leg, while my right leg rode shotgun on the passenger side, and my right buttocks sat on the emergency brake between the bucket seats. I did pretty good too, until I returned home, lost control in the driveway, went up and over the sidewalk, across the lawn and almost tore out a large brick planter. After that episode, I tried to live with the boredom. Doug also started hiding his keys.

One negative effect of a broken leg is that all the inactivity of the muscles causes them to atrophy just a little. I didn't have that much meat on my bones to begin with, and wasn't thrilled with the aspect of losing more. When my final cast came off, my right leg was a pale scrawny thing compared to my left, which had been picking up the slack. Now you would think that eventually the right leg would catch up with the left, but for some reason there was a misunderstanding, and between the two of them, they decided that it would be a lot easier for the left leg to lose weight, than the right leg to beef up. My little chicken legs got even smaller and my tipping over became more frequent.

Over the decades I've fallen out of trees, off roofs, ladders, barns, and hay lofts. I've had innumerable bicycle and motorcycle crashes, two of which left damages to the other vehicles that were caused by my body smashing into them. I've busted three out of four major appendages, a passle of fingers and toes, a handful of ribs (on separate occasions), had two or three concussions, several surgeries, and collected enough stitches to make a decent quilt. By the way, stitches are preferred over broken bones, because they leave you with really cool scars. Old scars are like medals of honor, something to be proud of. Old broken bones are like an old tractor, they're real hard to start on cold mornings, and nobody but you seems to care whether you get them going or not.

My morning routine these day's, requires an hour of hot coffee and a lot of slow moves for the beat up bones to even consider catching up with the few good ones that are left. It's not a great routine, but it seems to be all I have.

I've had people tell me that I'm an accident waiting to happen, but I don't believe this to be true. I have merely chosen to expose myself to many things that the majority of people would not. It has always been my belief that if you are afraid of dying, you are also afraid of living. I have lived, have the scars to prove it, and will continue getting them. Death means nothing more to me than a chance to be horizontal for a little while, and give these bones a good rest.

Many people like to compare themselves to a mighty oak tree, being tall and strong. I like to compare myself to a mighty dandy-lion, poking its head up through a crack on the freeway. Sure, I get run over a lot, but I keep getting back up, although it takes a whole lot longer on really cold days.

THEY CALL ME
"MISTER MOONER!"

Over the years a boy gets saddled with many nicknames. Some are deserving and make sense, others do not. The first nickname I ever had was **Pearl Pue**. I don't honestly know where it came from, or who gave it to me, but I'm guessing it was either my twisted sister, or my twisted mother. I continue getting called it to this very day. It use to haunt me, but it's been around for so damn long, that it has become a welcome sound.

Oft times nicknames get started by changing the name around. Friends, family, and foe, took Dave, and switched it to names like, **Davy, Davy Crockett, Davy Jones** (first it was the guy with the locker, then it was the singing monkey), **Dahveed, D.W.** and of course, **Dipsh_t**. Now in all honesty, you have to add and drop a whole bunch of letters to get **Dipsh_t** out of Dave. They then took my last name of Whiteman, and came up with the obvious, **Whitman, Whitehead, Whitewoman, Whitey, Weazelbutt** and, (once again, using an awful lot of alphabetic poetic license) **Dipsh_t**. From there you go through life wondering what your next moniker is going to be and how you will get it.

In high school I was on the gymnastics team. After working out on the rings one day, I was dubbed **Armpit**, or **Pit** for short. I'd rather not talk about it. I was later given a necklace with that name on it. **Pit** isn't a great nickname, but there were worse. One kid, who was our best hope for floor exercise, had a natural walk that was kind of a cross between a type A penguin and a drunken chipmunk. His nickname was **Sperm**.

118

Shortly out of high school, I was doing yet another stint of farming. Every day or two, I had to deliver produce to the stores in town. At the crack of dawn, on route to the stores, I would drive the big truck to various houses, making anonymous drops of fresh produce. *Pit* was gone, and now at the wheel was the **Phantom Farmer.**

During the early years of a troubled marriage I reached a point where I was in desperate need of some fresh air, so I went thumb riding with Chicago in mind as my eventual destination. En route however, I stumbled onto a little Lake Resort alongside the Platte River in Nebraska. At best, it was a funky oasis in a very strange desert. Just my cup of tea. They offered me work, free grub, and a tent to sleep in, so Chicago went to the back burner. I did fix-it work around the campground/resort all day, and spent the nights-tending bar at the lake's lounge. There were many people who lived at this campground not only all summer, but a few all year round. Some of them were legitimate, some were kind of in hiding, while others just had no place else to go.

There was **Doc**, who at the time, was a doctor and also head cook and owner of the resort. He was a big pot-bellied man, with a handlebar mustache, who had a very unique customer service philosophy. **Doc** told us that we owned the place, and if we didn't like the looks of anyone, just throw em out, period. One day a camping patron came up to **Doc** and myself, to lodge a complaint. He very politely said that his wife had spotted a spider in the shower house that morning, and thought that we would like to know about it. **Doc** calmly said "*Tell your wife we don't want her camping here ever again*" and walked off into the kitchen. Done, finito, end of discussion. The guy looked sympathetically at me and said "*Well, I never!*" I told him "*And apparently,*

119

you never will here again."

There was ***Tattoo Doc***, who never was a doctor, but use to ride with the Gypsy Jokers, or the Jolly Rogers, and had tattoos covering his entire body. He was our head of security at the campground. ***Tattoo Doc*** was the first man to ever kiss me square on the lips. It came quite out of the blue, and with a laugh, he was gone. While I was spitting for my life, I was told by someone else that being kissed by a biker was quite an honor. They said it meant that I was accepted, one of them so to speak. Won't that look good on my resume, Oh joy!

There was ***Weird Al***, who was without a doubt one of the strangest people I'd ever met. He'd been everywhere, done everything, and knew everything there was to know about anything, particularly treasure hunting. He was going to be a rich man as soon as he could get together enough gas money to get out of town. One early a.m. found a bunch of us sitting around the campfire, having a few drinks and relaxing after a long days work. Suddenly I saw, a bunch of sparks, reflecting off of the lake, and coming down the highway. Something was approaching, and it had sparks flying thirty feet up and out of it's rear end. I was in a state of mind that made me think it was the apocalypse, but it just turned out to be ***Weird Al***, who had blown a rear tire twelve miles back, and chose to drive the old Pontiac home on the rim.

There was also an old guy who went by the name of ***Dirty Al***. I don't think he was related to ***Weird Al***, but I'm not sure. I don't recall that much about him, but in spite of the fact that I showered daily, and he didn't, they started referring to me as ***Dirty Dave***. Maybe some thought we were kin, I don't know. They found him that following winter froze dead underneath a tree. I guess he finally had someplace to go.

I spent the following six or seven winters working at a grocery store in the Sierra's. For some reason the Assistant Manager thought I reminded him of some nightmare from when he was in the military, and pegged me with **Boot camp**, or **Boot** for short. I eventually got a custom license plate for my car that read **YO-BOOT**. **Dirty Al** and **Dirty Dave** were now both gone.

A few years after that I was back in Oregon, working at a grocery store in Albany. After work one night, I grabbed a six pack of beer and headed to the check-stand. After my purchase, a sixty-year-old woman followed me through the check-stand, and full length of the front lobby. Every few seconds, I could hear her muttering something that sounded like "*young man*", but I was in a hurry and chose to ignore her. I kept walking, and she kept muttering, until I got outside of the store when she finally said "*YOUNG MAN*" loud enough to get my attention. She then commenced to inform me that my pants were ripped out from my belt all the way down to my crotch.

Now for reasons that I won't even try to explain, this was at the tail end of a thirteen-year period of time, where I didn't own, or wear, underwear. I reached back, and grabbed a handful of hide, thus verifying what the nice old woman had just told me. I tipped my hat, thanked her, covered up the problem with my six pack of extremely cold beer, and chuckled all the way to my truck and all the way home.

Good-bye **Boot**, Hello **Mooner.**

PANTS

In the beginning, there was cotton, and then sometime during the mid 1800's, Levi-Strauss came up with denim. One hundred years later, my folks put themselves and their five Tasmanian devils through enough denim to carpet a small country. You would be hard pressed to find anything that will withstand the rigors of hard living, as will a pair of Levi's, but can you imagine paying the bill when your buying them a dozen at a time?

My mom sold Levi's at a feed store during the sixties when they were a fair trade item and had a suggested retail of just over three dollars a pair. I recently finished school shopping for my three sons, and I can attest to the fact that they are no longer three dollars a pair.

The feed store would deduct all of my mom's charges off of the top of each month's pay. This made her ending gross pay less, and therefore she had to pay less taxes. Between keeping herself, her husband, and their five offspring in boots and Levi's, plus charging feed for the menagerie of goats, chickens, turkeys, cows, horses, dogs and hogs that were running around our backyard, my mom's net pay would sometimes hover right at zero. Kind of a good news/bad news scenario.

Just in case the IRS is reading this, I would like to make the following statement;

THE PRECEDING PARAGRAPH IS COMPLETE FICTION! MY FAMILY IS AS HONEST AS THE DAY IS LONG, NOT, I REPEAT, <u>NOT</u>, AS CROOKED AS A DOG'S HIND LEG, AS SOME MIGHT HAVE YOU BELIEVE!

There, that ought to do it.

When I was in grade school, one of the worst things that would happen to me would be those rare occasions when I would accidentally destroy or lose my pants. This was far worse than flunking tests or getting beaten up by bullies, all of which happened fairly often. I would wake up in the morning and inform my mom that I had no pants for school, explaining to her that I didn't know where they went. I had taken them off when I went to bed, and come morning they were gone. The search would begin, and eventually my mom would come to grips with the fact that I really didn't have any pants left. You can only imagine her joy, as she would get the other four kids off to school and then drive me into town to charge a brand new set of Levi's at the feed store.

The trouble came from the fact that there was no time to wash them, so I would have to show up not only late for school, but wearing shiny new armor. There are few things as comfortable as an old pair of Levi's, and nothing as uncomfortable as a new pair, except possibly having a porcupine in your pants.

The pants were so stiff that I could hardly sit down in them and so coarse that they practically rubbed the hide off of me as I walked. The kids at school enjoyed taunting me for several reasons. I was not only late for school but I was also wearing pants that were way too big, and the cuffs were rolled up. The cuffs had been rolled up from when my mom adjusted for proper shrinkage and I had forgotten to unroll them upon arriving at school.

I think my mom would buy me pants that were too big for two reasons. One; she had to allow for shrinkage. Two; Levi's were so durable that I think she would speculate on how much I was going to grow in the next two years, and then get them big enough for that alleged growth. The normal shrinkage on a pair of boy's Levi's is a couple of inches in the inseam, and up to an inch around the waist. I had to show up to school wearing pants that were not only twelve inches too long in the legs, but had enough extra room in the waist to fit a porcupine.

At this point I think I need to make one thing clear. Any references to porcupines are just a figure of speech. I did a lot of stupid things growing up, but I was smart enough not to put wild animals in my pants. Well, at least no porcupines anyway.

There was one other problem that came with my mom buying me oversized pants. If they were large enough for either of my older brothers to fit into, then they would steal them, leaving me once again with no pants to wear to school. Its no wonder I had so many nightmares about showing up to school with no clothes on. Looking back on it now though, I kind of miss those early morning trips to the feed store with my just my mom and I. She could give Mother Theresa lessons in patience.

In the early seventies, I broke my leg skiing, and was forced to wear bib-overalls to high school. The other kids liked this alternative look so much that it became quite a fashion trend. Part of the intrigue with the look came from the fact that the youth movement was trying to buck the establishment and wanted to get back to the land. But you can't convince me that deeper down, that same group of new found bib-overall fan's, weren't equally intrigued by all the hammer loops and the plethora of pockets.

Around that same time, Brother Doug found himself en route from Oregon to Connecticut. He was taking a much-needed sabbatical from tree planting, and was clad in pants and shirt that he had made out of tent canvas, and had hand sewn together with dynamite fuse. This was around the same time of D.B.Cooper's historic hi-jacking, so it surprised my folk's, when airport security actually let Doug board the plane. That was probably the first and last time, which this particular fashion trend ever flew. However, since Doug is the only person I've known to have actually worn clothing made from an old tent, using dynamite fuse for thread, I guess you wouldn't really call it a trend, so much as you would probably just call it unique.

But wait a minute, isn't a unique, one of those guards at a harem? No, no, no, my mistake, that's a eunuch. Kind of makes you wonder however, if that eunuch didn't become a eunuch, because he was wearing pants sewn up with dynamite fuse, and maybe an errant cigarette touched off his trousers? It could happen. And what harm would befall the porcupine? Hmmmm?

Just out of curiosity, am I the only one who asks these kinds of questions?

I was afraid so.

PEARLS OF WISDOM

Advice is something that a person receives a lot of over the years. It is almost always given with the best of intentions, usually unsolicited and also very seldom used. Advice is very similar to squash from someone else's garden. Everybody seems to have more of it than they care to use, and therefore pass it on to everyone who may or may not need or want it. Most advice, like unwanted squash, usually winds up in the mulch. Although periodically, something takes root in that steamy pile and you put it to use.

My dad use to tell us kids that if a man calls you a fool, don't be in a hurry to open your mouth and prove him right. These are words to live by. I don't, but I probably should. It would save me from eating a lot of crow, which I am not that fond of.

My mom always told us that if you watch your pennies, the dollars would take care of themselves. I've watched my pennies, and the dollars did take care of themselves to the extent that they left home A.S.A.P., leaving me with a pocketful of useless copper. But seriously, it was still very sound advice that really does work. I don't have much, but I know that I would have even less, without using my mom's advice.

A couple of years ago I asked my sister if our childhood was the way I remembered it. She told me that our childhood was <u>exactly</u> the way each of us remembers it. I cocked my head sideways at first, and then the light went on over my head and I understood what she meant.

My older brother Doug once wrote: "*Feel free to come and sit inside my hut, but if indeed your mouth grows tired, feel free to keep it shut!*" Doug takes after his father and doesn't mince words. A long time ago, my kid brother and I were at one of Doug's wrestling tournaments. We were playing catch with a basketball, in the hallway outside of the main gym where the tournament was being held. At one point, a couple of older thugs took our ball and started playing *keep away* with it. We were frustrated over not being able to get our ball back, when I noticed my brother Doug jogging down the same hall.

It was not unusual to see wrestlers running between matches, so the thugs paid no heed to this particular ninety-eight pound jogger. However, even though Doug was much smaller than they were, when Doug got in the same vicinity as us, he grabbed the guy with our ball by the chest, slammed him into the wall lockers and calmly, but firmly advised him to give the kids their ball back. The ball was instantly returned, and Doug resumed his jogging. The thugs never did know who the jogger was, or that he was related to the two boys' with the basketball. They did know however that there was something in the little jogger's eyes that told them not to mess with him, or the boy's, and they didn't.

A few years later, as a teenager, I was visiting my oldest brother Jim who was in the Air Force. Jim and his wife took Dan and I to a motorcycle race. After the race, we were walking through the parking lot when an impatient car kept nudging it's way forward trying to part its way through the crowd. Unfortunately the driver made a large lunge while Jim was walking by with his new bride and his two younger brothers. I watched Jim spin around and kick the front of the car. The car stopped dead in its tracks. Jim's boot had given the car some sound advice, and the car apparently fully understood.

A dozen and a half years later I was living in the Sierra Nevada Mountains and scrimping for wood to survive the long, cold winters. My kid brother, Dan, had shown up from a stint of falling trees down around Orroville, Ca. We visited for a piece and soon got on the subject of woodcutting and chain saws. He offered some much-needed advice on the care and maintenance of the little chain saw that I owned. He also offered to help in my wood gathering the next day.

We went out early the next morning and I explained to him that the forest regulations strictly prohibited the falling of tree's so we had to limit ourselves to windfalls and slash piles in our search for wood. He gave me some more tips on my chain saw, got me started on a nice slash pile, and then told me he was going to wander a little deeper into the forest.

I was very proud of my little saw and fairly impressed with the little logs I had been chewing up with it. I was particularly impressed with the degree of sharpness that Dan had put on my chain. When I was finished cutting my pile, I loaded the wood, and proceeded into the forest in search of Dan. I rounded a bend in the trail, in my old Willys pick up, to see Dan dropping about a sixty foot Ponderosa Pine snag onto the road. His saw was about three times as long as mine was, and the tree he was falling was ten times as long as anything I had been whittling on.

What impressed me the most was that Dan had never once said anything derogatory about my little saw, and he actually went off to fall big tree's, without me watching, so as not to make me feel embarrassed or inferior. Oft times the most important words are those unspoken.

COLD

In the early seventies, Brother Doug was spending the winter in a three-walled shack, located in the Coast Range just out of Seal Rock, Oregon. Now I know what you're thinking. Your thinking that he lived in a triangle. Well that is where you would be mistaken. It was indeed a square shack with three walls. It's just that the fourth wall (that's the one that was both there and not there, much like our own fourth dimension) was made out of visquene. It was kind of like having a giant picture window for a wall, although you couldn't see through it real clearly. And depending on your ever-changing frame of mind, the figure you might see walking by the window, could be a bear, bigfoot, or just Burly Bob the Butcher from Brazil, who lived in a big brown bi-level bungalow behind my brother.

All right, that part is a lie. There was no Burly Bob. I just got carried away with the B button. I'm sorry. I'd like to tell you that it won't ever happen again, but I think that you and I know better, now don't we. By the way, did I tell you that Burly Bob drove a beat up blue Buick. OOPS, there it goes again.

Anyway, while this visquene wall made the shack extremely cold and drafty, it also added a certain ambiance. There is nothing quite like living in a shack in the woods to get you in touch with where you stand and what you have in the world. Where you stand is usually near the woodstove, and what you have in the world is generally lying on the floor next to you. As a rule of thumb, the smaller the floor, the less you have. What you do have will fit on your back, and consequently, the freer you become. This is one of life's paradoxes. The more you own the more your belonging's control you. If you can't give it away, you no longer own it, but it owns you.

Doug once told me that he wanted to be either filthy rich, or dirt poor. He wanted to have it all, or none of it. His reasoning was that either way you had the same amount of freedom. It took me a while, but I eventually understood what he meant. While the rich man can go skiing in Norway, a poor man might be sliding on his butt down a hill in the Sierra Nevada's. At the same time that the rich man is contemplating the temperature and texture of a certain bistro's cuisine, there is another man dreaming of a burnt bologna sandwich while he's digging ditches in Nebraska. While the rich man is wondering which wine will best cleanse his pallet, the poor man knows that true hunger makes all food the best he's ever tasted. The poor man also finds solace in knowing that when he is done with that sandwich, the stars above are for everyone's enjoyment.

My son Sean asked me the other day, what was the coldest I had ever been? I didn't answer him right away because I didn't really know. A few days later however, I started to remember. It happened in the seventies, while I was hitchhiking with Brother Doug. We were in New Mexico and heading to Oregon. Just before leaving New Mexico, I had met a couple of little boy's who were traveling with their unemployed father. I didn't own much of anything at the time, but they obviously owned even less. The boys were entranced with my backpack and the sleeping bag I had attached to it. They were living out of their car and the sight of a backpack and sleeping bag seemed pretty exciting to them. So I gave one of them my sleeping bag. Doug in turn gave the other boy his bag as well. Sometimes children need Christmas presents out of season.

Doug and I left Farmington, New Mexico, that same day, or the next. I really can't remember but two or three of the rides that we got. One ride came from a couple of Navajo girls driving a Ford pick-up. They wound up taking us to a drive-in theater. I can't recall the movie that we watched but I do remember that the girls smelled a whole lot better than the popcorn.

Another ride came from a married couple driving a flat bed truck with side rails. They told us to throw our gear in the back. When we got to the back of the truck I could see that it was almost full. There was a washer and dryer, a half dozen boxes of groceries, some hay and feed, a big dog, some chickens, and a half dozen barefoot dusty kids. Doug and I rode with our legs hanging off the back of the truck, while the kids asked us all sorts of questions about traveling. They were a good group of people, and one of my favorite rides of all time. I took a liking to one of the barefooters and gave him my harmonica when they dropped us off.

Later that day found Doug and I alongside a barren stretch of road, still heading west. There were very few cars on the road, which made for lousy hitchhiking. It was so bad that I reached a point where I crossed the road and tried to catch a ride east, while Doug kept trying west. My thinking was that it was better to get a ride heading **somewhere**, than to **not** get a ride heading to where you thought you wanted to go. As it turned out, neither Doug nor I could catch a ride heading anywhere that evening. Of all my travels, this was the longest dry spell I'd ever had.

We watched the sun go down on our thumbs and with the sunset came the realization that we were there for the night. We walked up to a little rise just above the road, and curled up into our respective coats. Not many words were spoken, but I'm sure we were both wondering when our next ride would come, and what our next meal might be. I have no way to tell how cold it got that night, but I remember waking up every twenty minutes or so, in the death throes of some of the worst cold shivers I have ever experienced. At least a half dozen times during that night I reached into my backpack, found my survival matches, and made a little tiny bonfire of atlas pages and sagebrush. I would warm my hands on the little tiny rip roaring belching hell of fire, and then lay back down and doze off for another twenty minutes or so, until hypothermia would once again tap me on the shoulder, telling me to move it or lose it. Since I didn't want to lose it, I would get up and repeat the fire drill.

My time on life's road has taught me many things. You don't appreciate heat until you have had none. It's hard to complain about any food when you have contemplated road kill. And you don't spend a great deal of time speculating on a wine's bouquet, when you have drunken from many of life's ditches.

ROAD KILL

A very special lady once asked me if I had really been hungry enough to consider road kill for eating purposes. Let me clarify something here. She didn't just blurt out *"So, have you ever eaten road kill before?"* She asked the question because she had just read a story I had written, where I wrote of being hungry enough to contemplate eating road kill. She was naturally curious as to how much truth there was in that statement. I had to reach way back into my mental attic before I could truthfully answer her question.

It was a summer day in the mid-to-late sixties, and I was riding my bicycle home after some farm work. It was my habit to scan the ditches along the highway for empty beer or pop bottles, pick them up, and eventually take them into town for the cash deposit. On this particular day, the only thing of value that I spotted in the ditch, was a dead deer. I did what most thirteen-year old country males would do. I got off my bicycle, climbed down into the ditch, and inspected the deer very closely.

It was neither bloody, nor bloated. There were no flies hanging around it yet, and it was still warm to the touch. Its legs were still flexible so I knew rigor mortis hadn't set in yet. All of this told me that it had been struck and killed, quite recently. This was great news for a short scrappy scavenger on a Schwinn. I thought long and hard about all the options that lay in front of me. (*Who's kidding who here, there was only one option and that was to take it home. I figured that when my folks got off work, they could decide if they wanted to cook it or not. The worst case scenario was that I'd get a nice hide out of the deal. We already had one or two hides in the freezer, but there had to be room for one more.*)

I was only about a half mile from home and the thought of hauling the deer on my back was not very appealing. I had already put in a hard day and a deer gets mighty heavy when it still has a full belly. I didn't want to gut it there on the spot, as it would draw to much curiosity from the cars driving by. And then a light bulb went off over my head. Now granted it was only a 15-watt bulb, but it nonetheless went off.

It took a little doing but I managed to drag it out of the ditch and onto the edge of the highway. I drug my bicycle over to the deer and very strategically shoved it against the deer's underbelly. I stuck its head over the handlebars and shoved the bicycle seat into the deer's crotch. With both arms I reached underneath the deer and grabbed what I could of the bicycle. With my chin on the deer's back, I lifted with all my might. My plan worked. (Not necessarily on the first attempt, but it did work.) The bike was now on two wheels, with a deer as its passenger. I grabbed a handlebar with one hand, and wrapped my other arm around and under the deer's hind end until I could grab it's post. (*I'm talking about the post under the **bicycle** seat for crying out loud!*)

The deer was now on my bicycle with its head lying over the handlebars, it's butt sitting on the seat, and all four legs hanging down just barely missing the ground. I then walked the bicycle (while the deer rode) the half mile home. I steered it into the back yard and hung it from the grape arbor. After cutting its throat, I gutted it, hosed it out, and commenced skinning. I was halfway done with the skinning, when another light bulb went off over my head. (*Two light bulbs in one day would normally be considered a good omen, but this time paranoia had flipped the switch.*)

During the skinning, I had started thinking about how proud my folks would be about me getting the family some free venison. But then I started wondering if any of the cars that had driven by, might have taken offense by the spectacle and decide to turn in the boy with the deer riding his bicycle. We were well known up and down that highway, but not always well liked. It would be the perfect opportunity for some archenemy to turn me in for hunting out of season, without a deer tag, or a gun for that matter. I stopped skinning and started sweating. What to do, what to do? There was only one thing I could do. I had to call the police before someone else did.

I called the police and told them that I had found a road killed deer near my house and that maybe they should come and get it. Within an hour, an Oregon State Trooper pulled into my driveway. He asked where the dead deer was, and I took him out to the grape arbor and showed him. He looked at the deer and then at me, and then his head just kept going back and forth. When his head finally came to a rest, he asked me why I had gutted and skinned it. I told him that I had always heard that they fed road-killed game to prison inmates and I didn't want the meat to spoil.

At this point I have to explain something about my origin. My folks came from Colorado to Oregon almost fifty years ago. Somewhere between Colorado and Oregon it was common practice to use confiscated and accidentally killed game meat, for the purpose of feeding people in state institutions. That group of people were housed in prisons, asylums, and orphanages. Now before you get your Birkenstocks in an uproar, consider this. Times were different a half a century ago. The meat was not only free,

135

it was nutritious, and it would've otherwise gone to waste. I was raised believing that there are few greater sins than waste.

Anyway, the officer didn't say much after my comment about my concern with the meat spoiling. He just had me cut it down and he helped me haul it out to his patrol car. I thought he was going to put it inside of his trunk, but instead he just threw the deer on top of his trunk. He gave me an odd look, got into his patrol car, and drove off to town. What he did with the deer, I really can't say. I can tell you however that the meat was still good for eating. Most people might not want to eat it, but I've eaten worse.

I was disappointed, because I had really hoped that by my being semi-honest, I would have been rewarded with getting to keep the deer. I was however, equally relieved over the fact that he didn't pull out his handcuffs and haul me off also.

But wouldn't it have been ironic, if I had gone to jail for taking a road killed deer, only to wind up eating it a few days later?

SHESHBETAH

In the late 1940's, my parents went to work on a Navajo reservation in Chaco Canyon, New Mexico. They worked for my Uncle Glen, who owned the trading post on that reservation. Glen paid my parents one hundred dollars a month plus room and board. The trading post was a stones throw from the famous cliff dwellings of the Anasazi (*The Ancient Ones.*)

My folks had with them a newborn daughter that the Navajo people just loved to come to see and to hold. To many of the Navajo this was the first white infant they had ever seen. This white infant that drew their curiosity was my sister Linda. She has since grown up, and like her four brothers, still draws much curiosity to this very day.

Linda was new enough that my folks used to put her in a small box placed between them, when they went for rides in the desert. They used to take off across the desert in an old Model A pick-up and do some rabbit hunting. As the old Model A would bounce across the arojo's, Linda would bounce around in her little box. Forty five years later has found Linda still bouncing around in the high desert, but old enough to giggle about it all now.

My folks learned much of the Navajo language, which at the time, few others knew. I have since learned that the U.S. Government used much of the language during W.W.II for secret codes since there was no written version during that time. My Uncle Glen lived and worked with the Navajo for most of his life, and is a pure joy to listen to. It is truly one of the most beautiful languages ever spoken.

My mom has told me of looking out of her front door to see the Navajo in full dress, tethering their horses on the top of the mesa overlooking the trading post. It would take the Navajo a half-hour or longer to make the treacherous hike down from the mesa to the trading post. My mom was a shy little red headed girl, and was naturally intimidated by the Indians in the beginning. Most of them had never seen a girl with red hair and freckles before, so I suspect that they were as nervous as she.

My mom and dad didn't speak a lot of their language in the beginning and consequently there were often times some gruff confusion over what their trading intentions were. Many of their words, if misunderstood, had vast differences in meanings. Most of the time Glen was there to help with the translating, but on occasion he wasn't. My mom and dad at this point had to fend for themselves. They did this with the best grace and dignity that two teenage parents could.

Many decades later found me bringing my wife and my infant son, for a visit to my folk's house. We had driven 700 miles to spend Christmas with my family, and my mom had made all sorts of food and sweet treats that were spread out all over the place. One treat in particular, was a fig or date roll, that was about two-thirds the size of a hotdog. My dad happened by while my mom was putting a plate of these things onto the buffet. He stopped dead in his tracks, shook his head and with a little grin said *"SHESHBETAH, It looks like SHESHBETAH, I hope it tastes better"*

My mom clobbered my dad in mid-flight.

In the Navajo language that my parents grew up with, **SHESHBETAH** meant bear poop. And I have to agree with my dad on this one. It did indeed look like bear poop, but in my mom's defense, it tasted a whole lot better.

SEMI
HARDTIME

It all started at my son Sean's birthday party. Friend Tony and I were recounting various stupid things we'd both done while growing up, when the subject of stealing entered the conversation. From there Sean dug and dug and dug until he had pulled a full confession out of me. *Yes I had been arrested once, and no I wasn't proud of it.* A child badgers a witness far worse than Perry Mason ever dreamt of.

It happened while I was a young buck in Paris. I had fallen in love and made the mistake of stealing what I couldn't afford to buy, in my attempt to win the hand of a beautiful princess. Well, maybe that's stretching it just a bit. I haven't really physically been to Paris, although mentally I've been to more places than I can recall. I even get postcards from myself periodically, but anyway, I was in love with a beautiful princess, while I was just a young buck. All right, all right, she wasn't a princess, but she was really cute, and when you're in the sixth grade, that's right up there with being royalty.

So one day found me in a Gold Bond Stamp redemption store, and I made the mistake of stealing a full book of Gold Bond stamps from behind the counter and then trying to re-redeem them for a necklace for my girlfriend. You might call it another senseless crime of passion. What I didn't realize was that the store marked the books when they were redeemed, so I was immediately caught, the police were immediately summoned, and this twelve-year-old was immediately arrested.

The police possibly handcuffed me, (*I really don't*

remember that part) and put me in the squad car. With sirens blaring and lights flashing, (*I vividly remember that part*) they drove me the three blocks to the police station. The police station was an old converted railroad depot that to this very day just oozes charm and character. On that particular day however it just oozed nausea and thoughts of despair.

The police fingerprinted me, and then had me fill out a form that included my writing "*The quick brown fox jumps over the lazy dog*" in both printed and cursive form. They told me that this sentence contained every letter in the alphabet and now they would have my handwriting analysis on file in case of any future crime sprees. I suspected that these officers were in desperate need of being decaffeinated, but I was in no position to speak.

The police asked me whom I should call and I told them my mom. They snickered and implied that I was afraid to call my dad because I would get into even more trouble. I remember thinking to myself how stupid the police must be to think that my mom was any less feared than my dad, or that she could keep him from finding out about my recent exploit. Don't get me wrong, my mom was and still is very good at her craft, but this was a whole lot bigger than flunking some tests, getting my first traffic ticket or breaking a window.

Several years earlier, we brothers had broken a window and called mom at work to ask her what to do. My mom calmly asked us the dimensions of the window, called a glasscutter, had a pane cut, brought it home to us on her lunch hour, we puttied it in and the old man was none the wiser. Thanks to my mom teaching us window repair, on the other occasions that we would break windows, we bypassed mom, rode our bikes into town to get the glass, and fixed it ourselves. The old man was still none the wiser but nothing, and I mean **nothing** got past my mom.

Anyway, the police put me into a cell, locked the door, and left me to rot for all eternity, or until the arrival of my parents, whichever came first. There is a direct relationship between childhood trauma and the need for sleep. I lay down on that steel cot and fell asleep before I hit the **v** in "*My life is over.*"

When they woke me up to hand me over to my dad, I was surprised when he didn't kill me on the spot. But then I realized that there were probably law's against skinning your kids alive in a police station. It's probably a kind of hallowed ground type thing. So the way I figured it, he would probably dispatch me on the way home and sink me in the slough behind the house. I couldn't believe it. I steal one lousy Gold Bond book and the next thing I know I've got reservations for the cheap seats in the food chain. Dandy!

It was four miles from the police station to the slough behind my house. My dad didn't speak much on that trip and I handled the stress the only way I knew how, by once again falling asleep. When my dad woke me up, I was relieved to see that we were in our driveway and not down at the slough. He escorted me into the house, at which point my sister and brothers scattered like cockroaches do when the lights come on.

I was in for one of the longest, sternest, lectures of my life, and the two naps I'd had earlier, hadn't been enough, so I think I took a few more. This did not sit well with the warden or his wife, and naturally ruined my chance of early parole.

Three decades later, rumors have circulated saying that when my parents were informed of my crime, they told the police to run me through the wringer to teach me a lesson. That incident did indeed teach me a lesson. Don't get me wrong, it didn't stop me from doing stupid things. I had then, and still have now, an incredibly natural knack for doing stupid things. But I did learn not to get caught. Well, most of the time anyway.

DOUGMA
MORE SEMI-HARD TIME

Brother Doug was taking a break from his hitchhiking travels one year and renting a room in town. He had been thinking it would be nice to have a traveling companion so he got himself a dog from the pound and named him Mingo.

Since the dog squad in town didn't like loose dogs, and Doug didn't like leashes (animal or human) at first opportunity the Puppy Patrol apprehended Mingo. This was twenty-five years ago but it seems to me that the fine Doug should've paid was just under twenty dollars. The reason I say the fine Doug **should've** paid, is because he chose not to pay it, and that is how this whole twisted story begins.

I'm pretty sure Doug had the money to get Mingo out of the pound, I just don't think he wanted to retrieve his dog through conventional methods. He chose instead to leave his room in town one night and walk the four miles to our parent's house. He then went out to the tool shed, grabbed the old man's hoof nippers (for trimming horse hooves) and walked another half mile to the dog-pound. Under the cover of darkness, with the old man's nippers, Doug cut a hole in the chain link fortress that held Mingo prisoner. What Doug hadn't reckoned on was that his dog was not alone. As luck would have it, Mingo was sharing a cell with three fellow inmates.

The dog pound that Doug invaded that night, was located within a hundred yards of the airport, which also was less than a mile from the house we grew up in. The airport to this day still has one heck of a searchlight that runs twenty-four hours a day. The light rotates 360 degrees illuminating the fields all around it, and I do mean all around it. It lights up those fields every four seconds. I fell asleep to that night-light for the bulk of my youth. I recently had my son's time the light, and this is how I know its exact length.

After the breakout, Doug and Mingo ran across those fields, trying to hit the dirt every four seconds, which is no easy task in itself. The three other escaped dogs were following in hot pursuit. Since this was more dogs than anyone needed, Doug led the pack to the saw-mill parking lot which was halfway between the airport and my parents house.

There he found an unlocked pick-up and deposited the three extra dogs into its cab for the night. I can only imagine the look on the face of the pick-up owner, when he finished his shift at the mill, to discover what was left of the inside of his truck. The look on his face was probably very similar to the one that Doug wore the next day, when the police knocked on his door and arrested him for busting his dog out of the pound.

Now this wasn't the biggest crime this town had ever seen before, but it was the biggest one for our family. Not since one of my uncles had been arrested for riding his horse down main-street ropin garbage cans, had there been this much nervous snickering amongst the clan.

We all showed up in the courtroom for Doug's debut before the judge. Since he'd been arrested wearing nothing but cut-offs, the court had supplied Doug with some county coveralls to wear. They were of an orange color, and had numbers and letters stenciled on the back. Doug knew where he stood, and pleaded guilty. My family came from a long line of people who had to admit to a lot of strange things at various times, and this was no exception. My folks taught us to fess up when you're caught with your hand in the cookie jar.

Several summers later, I was between my own hitchhiking travels and back residing in that same town. Truth be known, I was renting the same room that Doug had been renting when he'd been arrested for dognapping.

One day Doug was riding his bicycle into town, (still wearing nothing but cut-offs) when he happened upon a red light at an intersection. There were no cars within a quarter mile, and he was experiencing one of those strange, torrential, summer downpours that Oregon is sometimes famous for. Because of these circumstances, Doug chose not to wait for the light to turn green, and rode his bicycle through the red light. This was reason enough for an over zealous cop to pull him over and give him a ticket for blatant disregard of a traffic signal.

Again Doug went to court, and again pleaded guilty. The court clerk told him to pay the twenty three-dollar fine at the appropriate window. Doug told him "*No*."

Knowing Doug as I do, I don't really think "***No***" is the exact terminology that he used, but the end result was still the same. They told Doug that if he did not pay the fine, they would have no choice but to lock him up. Doug told them to get to it, and they did just that. If memory serves me correctly (and it sometimes does) Doug was locked up for about a week.

Shortly after that incident, Doug resumed his wanderlust travels. His thumb carried him all over the United States for a large number of years. I don't mean an occasional trip out of town for a weekend, I'm talking traveling coast to coast, by thumb, for literally years and years. I have known my brother my entire life and I have never met anyone who has managed to squeeze in as much living in one lifetime as Doug has and still does.

For a few years following the dog pound episode I came into contact with the police on no less than a dozen occasions. Not for reasons that you may be thinking. Well, OK, a few of them were for those reasons, but most of the time I really was innocent. The point I'm trying to make however, is that each time I did come into police contact, upon their finding out who I was, they would inquire as to the whereabouts of Doug. A number of times a State trooper would even pull into our driveway and ask about Doug's location. My whole family learned to give vague answers such as "*Last I heard, he was either in Connecticut, or up on the Cimmaron. Would you care to leave him a message?*" They never would leave a message, so we never passed it on. Those were fun times.

One day (during the same summer that Doug did time for the traffic ticket, but three or four years after the dog pound incident) I was wandering around town with my girlfriend. We went into a shop and I left my dog outside. My dog's name was Goliath, and he was the spittin image of the Schlitz Malt Liquor Bull. Goliath was ten pounds of jet-black, muscle bound, and attitude.

Well I made the same mistake Doug had made years earlier and left Goliath outside, untethered. When I exited the store, a passerby told me that the Puppy Police had just moments before, hauled my dog off. I knew exactly where to look for Goliath. He was on his way to the same damn pound that Doug had busted his dog out of a few years earlier. I couldn't pay Goliath's bail until the next day, so my dog was going to have to spend the night at the pound.

I decided to take my girlfriend, and drive to the pound that night to say "*Hello*" to my canine friend. We drove to the pound, said our hello's, got back into my car and started

146

driving the three quarters of a mile back to my parents house. Halfway there however a police car pulled us over and then I noticed police cars flying at us from all directions.

I have never personally been involved with so many police lights before or since. I had one State Trooper, two city cops, and one County Mounty completely surrounding my car. And they were positioned so that I couldn't move forward, backward, left or right. Say what you want, I was both impressed and more than a little nervous.

One of the officers approached my car and asked for my ID. I gave it to him and then looked up into the night sky, figuring that with all the lights and security these officers were providing, Air Force One must be getting ready to land at the airport. The officer asked me who I had dropped off at the dog pound. I told him no one.

He was not only positive I'd dropped someone off, but he was insisting that the alleged person was my brother Doug. I told him that wasn't likely, because the last I'd heard, Doug was in Colorado herding sheep. The officer kept accusing, and I kept denying. I stuck with my story, only because it was the truth and all that I had. Eventually, they realized they had nothing to arrest me for and they let me proceed the final three hundred yards to my parent's house.

I spent that night at my parent's house and the next morning awoke to something scratching at the front door. I opened it, and who should run inside, but Goliath. I then got real damn nervous! I had an escaped convict licking my hand, roughly twelve hours after a lot of tax dollars had anticipated that I was going to bust him out.

I immediately got on the phone and called the pound. I told them about my dog getting arrested the day before, and how I was coming in that very morning to pay the fine, when I opened my front door to see my dog grinning at me. They told me that while they were cleaning the cages that morning, a few of the inmates bolted for freedom, with Goliath leading the pack. They also said that since Goliath had escaped their incarceration, that I was no longer responsible for his hotel bill.

You can call it fate, you can call it karma, or you can even call it dogma if you like. I prefer to call it Dougma, and I still firmly believe he was somehow responsible for the whole damn incident, regardless of which state (geographical or mental) he was or wasn't in at the time.

THE RUNNING OF
THE BULLS

In Northern Spain lies the city of Pamplona. Each summer the residents celebrate the feast of Saint Fermin, by running the bulls through the streets of the city to the bullring. Tradition has the young bucks of the city running in front of the bulls. The risks to the young men are maiming and sometimes death by trampling. As a young man, it had always been my dream to go to Pamplona and run with the bulls. Unfortunately, like many dreams of youth, this one never fully materialized.

In 1974, I was a year out of high school, had just completed a tour of the east coast, and had ridden my thumb all the way back to my home in Oregon. One June evening found me visiting a couple of my buddies at their apartment. I must have been feeling a little rambunctious that night because all of a sudden, and without warning, that dreaded light bulb went off over my head. My buddies spotted the light bulb immediately and even pointed to it.

They had known me long enough to know that I had just gotten a brand new idea. They also knew that while I do get new ideas periodically, they almost always spell trouble. (*I've learned to not only accept these idea's when they pop up, but to also turn loose of the reins just to see where the horse goes*.) I shared my idea with my two buddies and talked them into my own twisted version of **_The Running Of The Bulls_**.

I convinced a girlfriend to drive us to our old high school, where she dropped us off. My buddies and I then completely disrobed and threw our clothes into the back of her car. I instructed her to drive around to the far side of the football field and wait in the getaway car for our arrival. My buddies and I then commenced to streak the Senior Prom.

As luck would have it, the band was taking a break, so everyone was outside on the big cement patio, enjoying the cool night air. We ran through the 1974 Graduating Class of Corvallis High School, whooping and hollering *"**Class of 73**."*

We were weaving through the astonished crowd of several hundred, and everything was going fairly well. Anyway it was going as well as a streaking can go. I had instigated a handful of streakings back then, and they were all fairly similar. Basically you have to get naked and then run through a crowded place. I can even remember when the Oscars were privy to a streaking. It was on TV and David Niven was at the podium. He had the class to thank the streaker for showing his shortcomings to the world.

Anyway, the big difference this time was when one of the over-starched tuxedo clad males stuck his leg into my path, and I'll be honest here, **I don't think it was accidental.** Since I had been moving at a pretty healthy clip, (*streaking and strolling are not conducive to one another*) I went airborne. Now, I've been accidentally airborne many times in my life, but this was my first flight as a naked navigator.

As I was flying through the air, (*much like Superman, only without his protective suit and cape*) I realized that my landing gear (*I don't know what else to call it at this point*) was not only down, (*but also without wheels on it,*) and in immediate danger. After some very quick thinking, I resorted to some gymnastic wizardry, and turned sideways to minimize the damage to my landing gear upon impact.

As I skidded along the cement (*much like a flat rock on*

a calm pond) (*well, OK, you can't really compare it to skipping rocks on a pond. It would actually be more like throwing a side of beef off of a slow moving truck onto the asphalt, now that I think about it, and believe it or not I just did, and that alone is a very disturbing thought*) (*But anyway, if I can stop interrupting myself, I'll try to finish the sentence I started and left hanging at the beginning of this paragraph*).

But first, let's do a quick recap; I'm flying through the air, my landing gear is in jeopardy, I turn sideways, and then skid along the cement. That pretty much covers it I guess, so let's continue.

I slid to a crumpled heap, to the sounds of a sympathetic crowd. Apparently they had enjoyed the evening's surprise entertainment, and even collectively made a wincing "***oooooooh***" sound, as the soon to be limping streaker hit the cement. I'll just bet that made the jerk that tripped me feel like dirt!

Well of course it didn't. He was probably proud of himself. I could only hope that someday Karma would step in, and he would get his, particularly since he had almost cost me mine.

I picked myself up and limped away, still weakly shouting "*Class of 73.*" As it turned out I had removed a healthy section of hide from my right hip during the slide portion of the show. A couple of tuxedos chased us for a short stretch, but by the time we crossed the football field and made it to the getaway car, we were safe. Bleeding, but none the less safe.

That's the closest I ever came to running with the bulls in Pamplona. And that's OK with me, because it's still a lot closer then most people have gotten. And it's probably just as well. The way my life has gone, I'd have most certainly been gored or stomped like I've never been stomped before, and trust me I've known some stompings.

THE
MOUNTAIN

I had heard that there were no mountains in Nebraska. It wasn't until I made my own personal assault on one, did I find this to be untrue. I'm not saying I conquered it, but I did survive the attempt. In the foothills of my own mind, I can refer to it only as,

THE MOUNTAIN.

It often takes a bigger man to give another man a sound thrashing. I like to think it takes a spiritually bigger man to admit to being on the receiving end of that same thrashing. I personally know for a fact that it takes an incredibly naive man to really believe the old saying; *"The bigger they are, the harder they fall."*

During the summer of 1977, I was taking a hitchhiking interlude at a funky lake resort in a far off country that is today commonly referred to as Nebraska. The resort was located on the Platte River, halfway between Lincoln and Omaha. The Platte River was and still is famous for the amount of silt it carries along with it. The old timers say that the river is too thick to drink and too thin to plow. I can testify to that. The Platte is a bit of a paradox, because when you hear the word *river*, you think in terms of water. If you have ever seen the Platte, you tend to question whether it has any water content at all.

I swam in it a few times and each time I got out of the river, I noticed that my cutoffs had acquired about a handful of sand in each pocket. I usually swim to cool down from work. Since my work was equal walking distance between the Platte and the lake, I'm wondering now why I occasionally chose to swim in that muddy river as opposed to the cool clean lake. Silt for brains I guess.

The lake resort was a strange retreat full of strange people. It was called **Linoma Beach**, because it had a **beach** and it was halfway between **Lin**coln and **Oma**ha. The racetrack in Omaha was called **AKSARBEN,** which is Nebraska spelled backwards. Those Nebraskan's are a clever bunch, aren't they? I just referred to the resort as **The Ditch,** which in my mind is Nebraska spelled cattywompus.

The resort owner took a liking to me and immediately put me to work. I repaired and maintained the campground by day, and was bouncer/bartender at the very popular steak-house/lounge each evening. People drove from Omaha and Lincoln and would wait for an hour or more to be seated at our tables. We had a reputation for great food, and a certain bizarre ambiance that was unrivaled within the state, and quite possibly the free world. As the bartender, I had to keep these folks happy during their wait and keep the peace. The bouncer part of the job stunk, but tending bar had innumerable benefits.

. My first summer at the resort, I was loaned a tent trailer to live in. It was fine for sleeping in and kept me relatively dry during the famous thunder and lightning storms of that region. It even withstood my first tornado.

I had heard the warnings come over the radio, and watched as the twister put the boots to Omaha and then head towards the resort. I hopped into a truck and made a quick loop of the park, rounding up the campground guests. I told them to hole up in the lounge since it was made of cinder block, and was the closest thing to a real building that we had. After the roundup, as I walked the hundred feet from the truck to the lounge, the winds became so incredible that what started out as walking, ended up as crawling. I had to grab hold of poles and picnic tables as I crept towards the only safe haven in the park.

Once inside we all gathered at the bar, where the mood was pretty grim. It stayed that way until I said "*Drinks are on the house*" and the mood magically lifted. The tornado danced its way from Omaha to Gretna, went right beside us, headed on through to Ashland and then continued it's way to Lincoln and beyond.

The damage to the park was mostly just to our nerves. The lone exception being one fifth wheel trailer which had now had the top of a tree sticking out of it's roof like a TV antenna. Three hundred feet from where we had huddled, the twister ripped a forty foot tree out of the ground and dropped it several hundred feet further down the road.

However with the tornado gone, it was soon back to business as usual and we continued getting ready for the busy 4th of July weekend that was approaching.

The distance from the entrance of the resort, all the way around the lake, to the parks end, was one mile. Since there was a lot of family camping going on, we had established a park speed limit of ten mph. We enforced it by either yelling at the speeders to slow down, or occasionally hopping in a rig and going after them. If they were speeding leaving the park, we'd yell at them. If they were speeding coming into the park, they were ours to catch and to toss out. They couldn't get away, as there was only one way in and out of the park.

One night at around midnight the owners son, Brian and I were shutting down the lounge, when a speeder blew into the park. Before we could do anything, he had gone a quarter of a mile into the park, turned around and made the return trip doing about 45 mph. By the time we had hopped into Brian's Grand Prix, the speeder had left the park and headed down a gravel road that we both knew came to a dead end. Even though he had left the park (and was technically out of our jurisdiction) Brian and I decided to go after him.

When the speeder noticed our headlights in his rearview mirror, he did a quick turnaround, and came driving back our way. Brian blocked the road with his car and we both got out. We walked up to the now stopped pick-up and told the driver to stay out of the park. The driver very convincingly explained to Brian and myself that he was going to kick our butts. At that point he tried to open his door and climb out. The only thing stopping him was Brian and I pushing against his door in our attempt to keep him inside. We told him that there were children in the park, also that the park was private property, and we would call the police if he returned. At that point, this huge mountain of muscle successfully forced his way out of his truck, and repeated his earlier statement.

Brian and I looked up to him, not so much out of respect, but due to his altitude. We then looked at each other, and through some sort of mental telepathy, we jointly decided to **get the hell out of Dodge.** We told him we didn't want any trouble, we just wanted him to stay out of the park. The two of us jumped back into our car but before Brian could put it in reverse **The Mountain** started throwing punches at Brian's head through the open car window. Now in my mind, that's a sucker punch (which is right up there with sluicing ducks) and that was the only invitation this former kid wrestler needed, so out of the car I came.

I flew towards the front of the car questioning **The Mountain** about the marital status of his parents. **The Mountain** didn't like my comment, quit slugging Brian, and headed my way. Brian's eyes unscrambled long enough to see that I was about to die, so he put his car in gear and tapped **The Mountain** with his front bumper. While this maneuver did knock **The Mountain** off balance, it also made him all the more madder. He turned around and headed back towards Brian. By then I had reached the front of the car, and again questioned his heritage. This turned him once again towards me.

I flew at him headfirst, like a charging bull. Given the size difference, I was more like a charging Chihuahua, **but** a Chihuahua with a lot of attitude, and theoretically, with the powers of good on my side. My thinking was to head-butt him in the stomach, hopefully knock the wind out of him, and then get two points for a double leg take down. I figured if I could manage to get him into a full Nelson, I'd be in the money.

Unfortunately, **The Mountain** was not impressed with the airborne Chihuahua flying his way and with one roundhouse punch to the side of my head, modified my flight plan from my original destination. I did a perfect 90 degree directional shift that sent me sailing headfirst into the fender of his truck. What little I remember after that was Brian escorting me rather quickly into the back of his car and getting us the hell out of there.

By the time we made it back to camp we were laughing hysterically about the whole ordeal. The people at camp questioned us as to what had happened to our faces, since we had both received an assorted amount of black eyes, cauliflower ears, cuts, and bruises. I explained that Brian and I had just gotten the sh~t kicked out of us. The truth sometimes hurts, but it is always the best path.

The following summer I left Oregon and once again returned to **The Ditch**. I pretty much picked up where I had left off the previous summer, only instead of living in a tent-trailer with a hitchhiking buddy named Chuck, I spent the next three months living in a tent with my wife. Our refrigerator was a Coleman cooler that I had won for being the lawnmower salesman of the month, from my previous winter's job. It was a dandy. The cooler anyway, not the job.

That 4th of July weekend, I noticed a fight breaking out in the parking lot just outside the lounge where I was once again bartending/bouncing. It was my job to break these fights up and as I left the lounge I told the waitress that if she saw me go down, she better call the police. I pushed my way to the front of the crowd, and there in the dirt were two young bucks just beating the hell out of each other. Also standing at the front of the crowd was the same **Mountain** that had beaten the hell out of me the previous year; and he is rooting for one of fighters. Traditionally this is not a good sign.

I walked over to him and by jumping up, I managed to tap **The Mountain** on his shoulder. I told him "*You may not remember this, but you beat the hell out of me exactly one year ago today because you were speeding in my campground. Well, I'm here to tell you that I still won't stand for any trouble around here. Now what are we going to do?*"

The Mountain looked at me for about a minute, laughed and said "*Oh yeah, I remember you. Why don't you let me handle this.*" He then reached into the middle of the fracas, separated the two fighters and told them to knock it off, at which point they did.

I told him that I appreciated the way he handled the whole situation with such grace and dignity, and the fact that he hadn't felt obliged to beat the hell out of me once again.

I admire that attribute in people, I really do.

FOOD FOR THOUGHT

During their early years, my parents supplemented the feeding of their five closely grouped children, by reaping whatever bounty the land had to offer. Over the years this included everything and excluded nothing. My brothers and sister were very fortunate to have had our parents as our primary teachers in life. They taught us things that cannot be found in books. We could not have picked better role models.

When my parents moved us into the country, they knew that their offspring would require an exorbitant amount of food on a routine basis. Because of this, they planted a garden about half the size of the house we lived in, and also brought in fruit trees, grapes, berries and even currant bushes for their evil horde to feed on during the daylight hours. During the twilight hours we would often sneak out and raid the neighboring farms and orchards.

Apples, pears and peaches were exceptionally tasty by moonlight, but it was usually too dark to tell if they had any worms. Since hunger often outweighed fear, we would just hope that worms weren't present and continue feeding. After all, there are much bigger monsters than worms to worry about, in a farmer's orchard at midnight.

My favorite apple-picking container was a partially tucked in (long tailed) flannel shirt and a well-cinched belt. This technique allowed me both hands free to climb through the trees, (you have to go to the top for the really good fruit) while my tucked in shirt had a holding capacity of several dozen apples. The down side to this technique is that you look extremely plump and lumpy, but since the country was never intended for a fashion show there was little fretting done. It is critical that you cinch your belt as tight as you can stand it however or suddenly, and with little warning, your shirt tails will un-tuck and automatically unload it's precious cargo. This is bad news for both the picker and anyone climbing under him.

We soon discovered that cantaloupe was especially designed to be stolen under the cover of darkness, since you can tell if a cantaloupe is ripe by just rolling it. No eyes were necessary, because if the cantaloupe would sweat off the stem during the roll, it was ready for your gullet. If it put up a struggle, it should be left behind. It has been my experience that short of a kiss, there are few things as sweet as a moonstruck melon. It has also been my experience that if you have to force it from the vine, it is still green enough to give you a good case of the *green apple quick step*. I have found this to be true of both love and fruit.

My mom would can what was left from the garden, and whatever else we would glean from surrounding farms. Sometimes we would buy additional produce, other times we would trade labor for it, and occasionally we'd just leave home with an empty gunnysack, to return with it magically full. The produce fairy was always very good to us.

We also raised chickens, turkeys, goats, calves and hogs, all of which were destined, for our dinner table. After work at the sawmill, my dad would pick up garbage cans full of lunch scraps from my grade school to feed to his hogs. Let me clarify something here, my dad brought the scraps home for the four legged hogs, not the two leggers he lovingly referred to as his kids.

My folks managed to corral this collection of critters and carnivorous kids on just under two acres of land. It was a small piece of ground, but we kept every square inch of it productive. Even though at times it was only producing trouble, it was always producing something.

Of the many highlights while growing up on this micro-farm, the beheading of the chickens was somewhere near the top of the list. After the ax would fall, the chicken would run around like a chicken with it's head cut off (*OK, now I understand what that expression means*) and sometimes they would even try to fly, while their noggin lay silent on the block. It was always a race to see which boy would grab the chicken's head afterwards, and god only knows what he did with it once he had it.

The only time any one of us missed one of these cherished executions, was when my mom would hold us hostage in the kitchen. Her demands were simple and yet sinister. We either finished the green stuff on our dinner plate, or we couldn't attend the beheadings. Talk about cruel and unusual childhood punishment. I wonder if it's too late to get booked on Oprah.

Our cattle handled their demise much more gracefully than our chickens. My dad would give them a last meal of straw and molasses and then place his rifle between their eyes. They would make kind of an "***Erp?***" sound and then collapse, lunch still in mouth. They never did run around like a chicken with it's head cut off, which was an obvious disappointment to the band of bloodthirsty boys watching.

Out of the seven family members, five of us became avid and productive hunters and consequently, game meat played an important role through our long winters. Bird hunting and fishing is fun enough, but when you got down to brass tacks, venison was the hands down favorite for filling the freezer, as it was both abundant and large. When there was venison, there was venison aplenty.

Out of all of us that hunted, it was my mom who year

161

after year was the first one to fill her tag. It wasn't because she was a crack shot, (which by the way, she was and still is) it was because whoever got the first deer would fill mom's tag so he could continue hunting. Occasionally we would even call her at work to ask her to pick up a license and tag on her lunch hour and run it home since one of us had obviously been successful earlier that day. Nowadays this would be considered illegal.

Well OK, you got me, it was also illegal thirty years ago. However, in our defense, we had a large family and we wasted not one ounce of what we shot. We never trophy hunted, we all just contributed to the family as best we could, with full respect for all game taken. Quite often we hunted with another family in a similar situation to ours, and at the end of each hunt, we would split the deer equally, regardless of who shot what. We filled all tags but we never exceeded the limit. While we did bend the rules, we never stomped on them.

I can't remember how many times that our kitchen table sported a deer carcass on it. Mom and dad would be busy cutting and wrapping the deer for the freezer, while we five kids assisted as best we could. My favorite part of those nights were when my mom would take all the scraps from that nights meat cutting and chicken fry them up. There would usually be one or two huge plates of these nuggets for us kids to devour. Since most other nights we were on a house imposed meat ration, we all looked forward to a deer on the table, as we knew we got to eat meat until we dropped.

All of us that is, except our sister Linda, who sometimes went through spells where she wouldn't eat much meat. During these spells we all fought to sit next to her, with hopes of getting her abandoned share. It was very disturbing for Linda to try and eat, while her four younger brothers sat growling and ready to pounce, at her first mention of *"May I be excused?"* It's not a pretty sight watching four forks attack one little pork chop.

Once cut and wrapped, the deer would find its way into our freezer alongside an odd assortment of items, most of which were intended for eating. Besides an occasional deer hide or two, there was trout, bass, crappie, and catfish that were put into ice cube trays filled with water. Once they were frozen solid, they would be pulled out of the trays and stacked helter-skelter on the freezer shelves. It was a strange sight to open our freezer and see a half dozen bricks of ice, (with fish heads and tails sticking out of each end) staring back at you. The down side to this method of freezing fish was on those occasions that you would open the door and the fish bricks would do swan dives onto your feet. A troutsicle nailing your big toe to a cement floor is a very painful experience.

Fowl was good eating except on those occasions when you'd bite and then have to spit out, the same shot that originally killed the bird. Crawdads are exceptionally tasty although you can starve to death trying to get a bellyful. Frog legs do taste like chicken only because most of the time that's the way you cook them. Crawdads and frog legs both require a healthy amount to be anything other than an appetizer for a family of seven.

We built our own frog gigs (*toad stickers*) out of eight-inch long spike nails. We would hacksaw off the head and then beat the tip flat on the old man's anvil until it was a spearhead. We then used a bastard file to sharpen the tip and work a couple of barbs into it. Once that was complete, we would bore a hole (the same diameter as the spike) about two to three inches into the end of a shovel handle. We'd then take a hand saw and make a two inch deep cut, north to south and another cut east to west. The hole would be dead center of the **X** formed by the cuts. We'd then shove the shaft of the spearhead into the hole and secure by wrapping tightly with wire. If we wanted more heft and length, we'd have to whittle down a long piece of 2x2 until it was sort of round. The end result was a spear as tall as we were, with a very sharp, five-inch steel tip.

Now as I mentioned before, these spears were intended for frogs, but every once in a while temptation would get the best of us and we would practice our Zulu warrior hunting techniques. We had to be secretive and careful though, since we all knew that a dog, horse, cow, pig, brother or sister harpooned in the butt, would result in a severe whooping, Zulu warrior or not.

It's easy to hunt and spear frogs. You just find a good batch of still water, look for and aim slightly behind, their little eyes. Once speared, they don't run around like a chicken with it's head cut off, again much to a young boy's dismay. And when you pull up your spear, if you haven't worked a good barb into the tip, the frog will slide safely back into the murky water. Dead, but safe from us at least.

HAPPY TRAILS

It is easy to go where everyone else is going or has gone before, but it is often more rewarding to meander left and right while the rest of the world is heading down the straight and narrow. While the straight and narrow is very safe, it has been my experience that the best adventures come to pass on winding side roads. Given the choice between an old trail and a new one, I will usually choose the latter.

While following the herd puts you on a safe path, it is also both predictable and mundane. You quickly tire of staring at the south end of a northbound mule, and soon discover that it is much more enticing to break from the pack and blaze your own trail.

When you get lost (*and with any luck, you will*) at least your leading the herd, even on those occasions when you are it's sole member. The view while being lost, (*once you get past the panic*) is one of immense beauty and awe. What you see is yours for the taking, should you feel up to the adventure.

My grandfather homesteaded in Colorado prior to the depression and at some point during my youth it became my dream to do the same in Alaska. By the time I turned seventeen, I had contacted all of the correct government agencies, obtained the appropriate information and necessary forms, and was planning to head north after high school.

Unfortunately during my high school years (*as is often the case*) love blossomed, throwing a monkey wrench into my plans and thus catapulted me down a completely different trail.

Instead of homesteading on 160 acres of wilderness and fighting Kodiak bears part time, I resigned myself to working in an Oregon sawmill and preparing to settle down with my high school sweetheart. We were in love after all, and deep down I knew she had no intention of going to Alaska to wrestle bears. But again as life often goes, my high school sweetheart went off to college, fell in love with someone else, and left me high and dry during the winter of 1974.

Since I had also been entertaining some thoughts of hitchhiking the following summer, my mom suggested that I abandon the wait, quit work, and head out early spring. She told me to go while I could, since there would come a time in my life when I couldn't. I trusted her instincts, informed the mill that my green chain days were coming to an end, and commenced preparing for my upcoming journey.

I phoned my brother Doug who at the time was wintering in Connecticut. He had been riding his thumb for a number of years and I told him that I wanted to catch up with him somewhere on the road. Doug said to me "*OK, I'll tell you what, since I've never been to New Orleans before, why don't we both head in that direction and meet in about ten days on the corner of first and main at about high noon*" and then he hung up.

I got off the phone and told my dad that I was supposed to meet Doug in New Orleans in about ten days at about noon, on the corner of two streets I didn't know for sure even existed. My dad looked rather stern for a moment or two, and then told me to get back on the phone with Doug and make more specific plans. My dad then explained that since Doug had many years of hitchhiking experience to my

none, that I was at a definite disadvantage should anything go askew. This turned out to be very sound advice, since through all my future travels, askew always played a very prominent role.

I decided to take a side trail before meeting Doug on the East Coast however, and flew from my home in Oregon to Durango, Colorado. My dad's brother who owned a piece of ground in Ignacio called The Hardly Runnin Ranch met me at the airport. I stayed there long enough to shovel some horse stalls, visit some other kin, and have my head turned by a cute little redheaded cowgirl. Thanks to my veering off the trail heading east, I was staring into some mighty pretty eyes under a Colorado sky the same night that most of America was watching Hank Aaron break Babe Ruth's record. I missed seeing Hanks homer, and that's okay by me.

I eventually left Colorado and flew into New York City. From the airport Doug and his buddies hauled me to a little watering hole where Muddy Waters was playing. That was my first time in a bar, my first legal drink, and (*upon exiting the bar that night*) the first time I ever peed on a steaming manhole cover. While others were leaving their heart in San Francisco, I was leaving something else in New York.

Many years, thousands of miles on hundreds of trails, and countless manhole covers later, found me living in a cabin in the Sierra Nevada Mountains. While Alaska had yet to transpire it had also never left my thoughts.

During the winter of 1981, I invited an odd assortment of old friends and family to the cabin for a New Years Eve party. Some came from locally, some came from Oregon, and two of my brothers came from a part of Idaho that is so remote that the residents to this very day have never heard of New Years Eve, or manhole covers for that matter.

After a few days of much revelry and reminiscing, my brothers Doug, Dan and myself turned our thoughts once again towards Alaska and what it would require for all of us to caravan up there. We ciphered long and hard and came to the conclusion that life was too short not to try, and we all agreed to point our headlights to the far north come spring. For the next several months everyone collected data on border crossings, dog laws, gun laws and potential employment.

Brother Doug returned to the Sierra's one month later with some wind tunnel tubing that he had confiscated from an abandoned mine shaft in the Bitterroot Mountains in Idaho. He built a camper frame for my pickup and used the wind tunnel tubing, as it's outer skin. It was both lightweight and waterproof, and I gave him a half-gallon of Jose Cuervo Gold for his labor. As I write this, I realize how lucky I am to have had a brother that would drive a thousand miles (*and supply the materials*) just to build a camper for his kid brother, for basically no pay.

Brother Jim and my mom also drove fifteen hundred miles round trip to help haul things I would need en route to Alaska. Jim then spent several days replacing bearings and rewiring the trailer I'd be pulling north. He also designed and welded an apparatus that enabled me to turn my camper's plywood door into a small awning whenever I stopped for the night.

Every member of my family has done these sorts of things for one another over the decades and I would just like to tip my hat and say ***Thank you*** to all of them. My family never asked why any of us were doing anything, they just said "*Why Not*" and helped any way they could. A closer family you would be hard pressed to find.

Come spring I gave notice to my employer, only this time it was not just a job that was feeding myself, but the one and only job that was also feeding a wife and our two year old son. I left the Sierra's one early morning in a small pickup truck with a wife, a two year old boy, two dogs, two guns, a pocketful of twenties and hopes of rendezvousing with two brothers somewhere in Canada.

We did eventually meet and proceeded our way up the Alcan Highway. For the most part the trip went without a hitch until somewhere around Dawson, when we lost brother Dan who zigged when he should've zagged and wound up following his own side trail for several hundred miles.

There were four rigs pulling four trailers in our group, and each morning we would assign an eventual destination for the caravan to meet come evening. When Dan failed to turn up at that night's rendezvous, Doug backtracked for several hours looking for him. He found neither hide nor hair of Dan and eventually returned to camp.

Regardless of who misplaced whom, the bulk of us crossed into Alaska the next day and eventually took up temporary residence under a bridge just outside of Anchorage. We were excited about having made it to Alaska, but a little uneasy about having left behind a kid brother in the Yukon Territory of Canada. From our vantagepoint under the bridge however, we could see all rigs coming off the Alcan and we kept a steady vigil for Dan's 1957 Willys pickup.

We called our folks on occasion to let them know that we'd lost Dan and that if he should call, to tell him where we were. After a number of communiqués from all parties, we got a distorted version of where Dan was, and what had happened. My folks also informed Dan as to which bridge we were waiting under.

Dan rolled into camp after several days of wrong roads and backtracking. We all said our howdy's and then questioned him as to where he'd been. We also inquired as to why the door on his camp trailer was now deformed and tied shut with rope, since none of us remembered it being that way the last time we had the pleasure of his company.

Dan explained that by the time he realized he was on the wrong road, it was time to settle in for the night. The temperatures were hitting in the teens and twenties, so he and his dog went into his trailer and tried to light his heater. Dan was so road weary that he didn't notice the never before heard hissing sound coming from his gas furnace.

When Dan struck the match, he simultaneously heard a big boom and his dog yelping. One second later, he passed his own dog somewhere near the door, which he knew he had earlier shut, but was now mysteriously open. As it turned out, he had created enough of an explosion to not only blow out his trailer door, but a half dozen of the trailer's windows as well. The blast left one hell of a ringing in his ears, and his trailer didn't look quite the same, but Dan was thankful his eyebrow hadn't caught fire because he knew if it had, that he'd be dead for sure.

(*For anyone, who has never met my family, I have to explain that there are enough thick eyebrows in our group to weave at least one good horse blanket. And here is a little known family secret. In my parent's early years, money was so tight that they couldn't afford two eyebrows for each child. Consequently two of the four boys only got one eyebrow a piece. **BUT,** they are the kings of all eyebrows*).

Anyway, because of Dan's constant grinning while telling us about his little side adventure, I figured he was suffering from some sort of **PET. (P**ost Explosion Trauma) or maybe even **ICBIBUMTS (I C**an't **B**elieve **I B**lew **Up My** Trailer Syndrome)

But as it turns out he was just experiencing the aftershocks of **IMHBUMTB TNDIPUAFHITWW! (I May Have Blown Up My** Trailer, **B**ut **T**he **N**ext **D**ay **I** Picked **Up A** Female **H**itchhiking **I**n **T**he **W**ilderness, **W**ahoo!)

Proving once again that even those side trails are happy trails.

HAIR TODAY
Gone Tomorrow

I came into this world as a toehead. Somewhere along the way however, my hair turned into a grayer, thinner version of it's former self. What exactly happened I haven't a clue and it doesn't really matter. It is well known that over time, weather and elements will eventually turn a majestic mountain into a meager mound. While science may help to explain this phenomenon, the bottom line is that while you are looking at the former mountain, it is still presently just a mound.

Like many people, I was once not only younger but considerably cuter. I entered the world with blonde hair and as genetics fought to darken this color, my time spent toiling under the sun put up a good fight to maintain the light. The few pictures of my youth verify that I not only had blonde hair, but lots of it.

Recent photos paint a completely different picture. I have more forehead than ever before and my hair color has gone from blonde to brown to gray in what seems like a heartbeat. The potential for another ponytail also seems remote at best.

For some reason, I am reminded of a horse we once owned. His name was Kenny I think. Although it might have been Benny, or Jenny, or Denny, I really don't remember. His name was certainly not Lenny however. Lenny is my son Sean's grotesquely tattooed, puppet type monster that lives under my car seat. I would remove Lenny from the car myself but Lenny is evil and not one to mess with. Besides, with Lenny in the car, there is no need to lock it. Anyway, it doesn't really matter what our horse ?enny was called since he didn't answer anyway. (*I'm rambling again aren't I? Let me start over.*)

I am reminded of a horse we once owned. I'm hoping his name was Kenny. Kenny was black at birth, but soon turned all white. Horses do that sometimes, and so do people's hair. (*I'm not sure what (if any) value, the last two paragraph's have to this story but for some unknown reason our old horse ?enny jumped the fence into my mental pasture. I don't know why he showed up at this particular point, but I do know that he may be here for awhile, so just ignore him and let him graze.*)

Anyway, for most of my youth, my parents alternated being the barber to each of their four boys. We all sidestepped being first in line since it usually took one or two heads for the folks to get really warmed up. And because each of us boys regularly used and abused my mom's ever diminishing scissors collection, it was a rare day that a pair could be found at all, much less a pair that wasn't just dull, but didn't also have enough slop in them to slide a jelly bean through. These poor excuses for shears caused our hair to be pulled out at about the same rate as was cut.

We'd scream and jerk, as we'd lose another tuft of hair from our scalp, and our parents would holler back to quit squirming or we'd lose an eye or an ear as well. Usually mom would cut our hair while dad administered first aid. All told, it was a pretty good system. Out of the thousands of trips to the kitchen barbershop, only one of us four boys grew up needing not only glasses but a hearing aid as well. But with all due respect to my parents, it might not have been the haircutting that was to blame. (Just in case Brother Jim is reading this, I think I better help him out here.)

"I said it might not have been the haircutting that was to blame!"

(I wish I could remember if he has a good sense of humor or not.)

Growing up in the fifties and sixties was an interesting time for hair. For most of my youth our bathroom was well stocked with Butchwax, Brylcream and various other petroleum by-products designed to keep your own personal clear-cut, erect and shiny. Brylcream's motto was *"A little dab will do you"* but we figured if a little dab was good, a handful was even better. Our mom was the one that paid the price for this action and it was usually around laundry time. We four brothers greased up every morning and consequently every toothbrush, handtowel, bathtowel, bedsheet, pillowcase, and doorknob that fell into our path was the unfortunate recipient of hair grease. My big fear back then was that a fire would break out somewhere in our house and I would perish before my greasy little fingers could conquer the bathroom doorknob.

Looking back on it all now, it's small wonder that America's decades of devotion to greasy hair ultimately led to global oil shortages. The media blamed gas-guzzling cars, but the real source of the problem was hair products. You probably didn't know that did you. Well I did. I'm always thinking. Rust never sleeps, and I don't get much either. Hell, I've got idea's I haven't even thought of yet. (?)

In the early sixties the Beatles came across the big pond and somehow convinced America's youth to give up on crew cuts and consequently it became extremely popular to have longer, more relaxed hair. Most parents were not too keen on this trend and my dad was no exception. My brothers and I however, started looking into the mirror with just a little more curiosity.

As my hair started growing longer, I no longer wanted the axle grease look and tried to get by with just a combing.

My friends and I preferred to let our hair hang down in front of our eyes, and then flip it to the side (as needed) with a well-practiced headshake. This was all part of being **Cool**. The old man however, knew that **Cool** and **Communism** both started with the same letter and, **Consequently**, he insisted that I grease up each morning before school.

It didn't take too long however, for me to figure out that if I waited until the last minute to take my shower, my combed wet hair would create the allusion that I had used hair oil. The old man was happy, and by the time I got off the bus at school, my hair was dry and once again hanging in front of my eyes. Still **Cool** with a capital **C**.

The times they were a changing however and this game came to an end as the 1960's were coming to a close. I had turned sixteen, the Beatles were breaking up, the country was in turmoil (*not my fault this time,*) and my dad was pushing forty.

My older sister Linda had married, her husband joined the Army and wound up heading overseas. My older brother Jim was newlywed and the Air Force not only gave him free haircuts, but also very generously let him spend his first two wedding anniversaries between Vietnam and Thailand. And my next older brother Doug started a hitchhiking odyssey that would carry him not only away from barbershops, but also out of state and out of touch, for many, many years.

During this time my folks spent their evenings watching the news to keep an eye on Jim, and slowed down whenever they saw a hitchhiker on the highway, in hopes that it might be Doug. They never saw Jim on TV or Doug on the highway. For my parents, those were days where the phrase "*No news is good news*" was wearing real damn thin.

One evening the old man rounded up Dan and I for one of his sit-down conversations. I was sixteen and Dan was fifteen at the time. Since Dan and I were earning our own keep and paying our way through life anyway, the old man told us that he would no longer hassle us about our hair, or anything else we were doing for that matter. He said that he was proud of what each of his five kids had learned while growing up and since each kid had reached a level of self sufficiency, that he was cutting the reins on Dan and I. He told us that we were free to come and go as we pleased because it was now he and my mom's time. Looking back, I'm glad he was able to devote that time to my mom because, as it turned out, his time left was very short.

Many decades have passed since then. It is now the mid 1990's, most of the Beatles have returned to find that crew cuts are co-mingling with ponytails, and I can occasionally be found doing a little bit of haircutting on my own three sons. I'm no good at it, so consequently I only cut when they ask. Being a single parent, it's also up to me to administer the first aid afterwards.

A few years ago my oldest boy (Jesse) announced that he wanted to dye his hair. I told him that if he did, I'd shave his head. He said it was his right to dye his hair if he chose. I told him that while this may be true, it was also my right to shave it off, if I chose. Jesse countered with the fact that I use to have long hair. I responded with the fact that when I quit cutting my hair, it did indeed grow longer, but it never changed color overnight of it's own accord. He hasn't dyed his hair and I haven't shaved it off.....Yet.

It's become obvious that in many ways I have turned into my dad and that's OK by me. Right or wrong, we always knew where the old man stood, and I admire him for that.

In the long run, I only hope that I turn out to be half the man, parent, and friend that he was to all of us.

I know it took a lot for my dad to let his boy's have long hair. I also know for a fact that if one of us had dyed our hair green or purple, the first thing we would have seen would have been the old man smiling as he fired up the sheep shears.

The Write Stuff

I started writing my stories with no expectations, mixed emotions and mostly because of a simple request of a friend. The friend had asked me to put my experiences down on paper and I have done just that. These stories are of a special time with special people that I felt my three sons' should know about after I'm gone. However if by some wild chance I get thrown out of and have to return from, wherever it was I'd gone, what the hell, they can still read them.

One of the most commonly asked questions about my stories is if they are indeed true. You have to understand that the truth is at times a very strange and elusive target. I research my stories as best I can, but some of the characters are no longer living, some are in hiding, and the bottom line is that everyone remembers life from different angles. I think it must have something to do with how tall you are.

For many years of my youth, I drove around without a driver's license. These days I find myself commuting with poetic license. This means that when I use the number **FOUR**, it might actually have been three, four or five. It also means that when I refer to a person as Billy, his real name might have actually been Eddie. It's not unlike what happens at the end of certain movies and TV show's, when they say that the names have been changed to protect the innocent. The reason I use my brother's real names is because they were never innocent and are more than capable of protecting themselves.

I can honestly say however that ninety-eight percent of these stories are ninety-eight percent true. Which means that if I were a professional basketball player, I would be **GODLIKE** in terms of accuracy.

I will now take this moment to field a few questions from the audience. (*If you will notice, this is already a lie because I'm actually sitting alone at my computer right as we speak.*) (*And if your really sharp you will have also noticed that I have just lied again, since I am typing, and not really speaking.*) (*This is kind of fun because in all truth, neither you nor I know where I'm going with this story right now*) (*But just out of curiosity, are you getting as confused as I am with all these little half moon type things( )()( ) that are showing up all over the page?*)

Anyway I will try to answer some important (*or not*) questions. (*See, there they go again, popping up like twisted typewriter tulips*)

Did my older brothers Jim and Doug, sew me inside a gunnysack, haul me to the edge of the highway and convince me I was going to be run over by log trucks?

Yes they did. They were rotten to the core and will surely rot for all eternity from their actions. The mis-truth of that tale is that it might not have been log trucks. We had a lot of different Semi's rolling past our house back then, and while most had logs, some had other cargo. At the time my concern was not the payload so much as the proximity.

Did I really crawl into a nutria den carrying a big stick?

You bet I did. It would take a complete idiot to crawl into a nutria den without a big stick, and I like to think that I'm not a complete idiot. Although that raises the question as to what part is missing that would make me a complete idiot? I have just reread that sentence twice and I still can't tell if it requires a question mark or not? (Nor *that one*) (*Oh look, more tulips*) Maybe I could have a little help from the audience that still isn't out there.

OK, fine. Next question please.

Did I really haul a road-killed deer home on my Schwinn bicycle and then skin it while it was hanging from our grape arbor?

Yes and No. When Brother Dan read this story, he reminded me of the fact that none of my bicycles had ever been Schwinn's.

Did that same brother step off the roof of the chicken shed and land face down in chicken sh~t while trying to kill me with a basketball?

No he didn't. While reading of that particular event, Dan stopped mid-story and reminded me that he had landed on his back. I have since corrected the error.

During that same event, upon what I thought to be Dan's demise, did I really poke him in the ribs with a two-foot stick to see if he was still alive?

Maybe, maybe not. I may have just kicked him in the head, which is another tried and true method of checking whether an animal is dead or not. It matters not whether it was a stick or a kick, the outcome was Dan beating me like a rented mule.

Did my brother Doug go to jail for not paying a twenty three-dollar fine due to running a red light while riding his bicycle?

Yes he did. I'm just guessing as to the amount of the fine he chose not to pay, but I'll bet I'm within five bucks in either direction. And truth be known, I seriously doubt it was even his bicycle.

Did that same brother get arrested for breaking his dog out of the dog pound, and why did he do it?

Yes he did break his dog out of the pound. The only way I can explain as to why he did this, is that each of us brothers grew up knowing that we could either run for office, or run from the office. As luck had it, none of us leaned towards politics.

Did I have an uncle that was arrested for riding his horse down main-street, while roping garbage cans?

Yes I did. He was my mom's older brother and he didn't care much for politics either. He also did a stint riding the Mexican border patrol on horseback. We just haven't been able to figure out which town that the garbage can incident occurred. He's gone now and unfortunately took a lot of colorful history with him.

Did my kid Brother Dan, really blow up his trailer on our way to Alaska by striking a match?

Yes and no. Odds are that he didn't do it by striking a match. Dan always kept a few discarded disposable lighters around that were out of fuel but still had working flints. He used these dead soldiers to light his propane appliances. This utilized something that was theoretically worthless, but still had some use. This is not unlike myself if I think about it, and I just did, which is very depressing.

Did Brother Dan really hook me in the eyelid while chasing me with a fishing pole?

Indeed he did. He was trying to kill me at the time and he had also just shouted "*I'm gonna hook you in the eye you sun on the beach!* " prior to the hook sinking into my eyelid. Although in all honesty, I don't really remember if he said, "*Sun on the beach*" or not.

Many years' later brothers Jim, Dan, and myself went fishing for a few hours while the folks were cooking the thanksgiving bird. We were all standing in a rowboat at Gerber's slough when Dan cast a bass plug towards an overhang of bushes. For some reason the plug that was intended to be cast over my head, somehow planted two out of three barbed hooks into my back. I immediately screamed "*You hooked me in the back you sun on the beach*!"

After Jim and Dan quit snickering, they cut the line to the treble hook (which took some of the pressure off) and then cut my shirt all the way around the hook. This allowed me to take my shirt off so that they had a better view while cutting the remainder of the shirt (and my skin away) until the hooks came out.

I can live with back surgery in a slough, but they ruined a perfectly good flannel shirt in the process. You may think me a bitter person for this, but looking back on it all, I like to think that Karma made Dan's trailer blow up years later.

Who's snickering now little brother?

Am I going to continue to write these stories?

As long as these memories keep knocking on my door, I'll keep opening it and writing them down. As to the validity of the stories, there are not only plenty of witnesses and court records, but a whole bunch of mental and physical scars to prove all of them.

Hermit
One who lives alone and avoids the society of others.
A recluse.

There have been many famous hermits in my time. Howard Hughes and Gretta Garbo topping the list. Most famous hermits were fortunate to have had financial resources available to accomplish their desires. Case in point: Howard Hughes died a recluse billionaire. You can afford a lot of recluse with those kinds of resources. If I had had his money while he was sitting on a feather, we'd have both been tickled.

99.9% of the worlds recluses however don't have the monetary resources of the rich and famous. They are hermits by choice and only coexist with the rest of the world out of necessity. They understand that to a certain extent, they have to come in contact with other people, but they are not necessarily happy about it. While they are very creative about getting by with what they have, they also recognize that there are many things that they cannot make on their own. How often they come down off of the hill depends on what their necessities are and this is where the compromise begins.

If you feel that you need a car, than you also need gas, repairs, and insurance. If you feel the need for a boat, again you need these same things. If you feel the need for flying, just try to get by without most of the aforementioned. Many people depend on vehicles to take them away from where they are, and to get them to where they think they want to go. Unfortunately most miles put on a rig, are miles taking you to and from work.

The hermit questions whether the juice is worth the squeezing.

I figured out once that it took almost 25 % of my yearly earnings to maintain a vehicle to get me to and from my job. I'm not talking about a Yuppie-mobile, I'm just talking gas, repairs, and insurance, on a basic rig. That means that almost one and a half days out of every week's work is spent justifying a stupid car. I can only assume that justifying a smart car takes even longer.

Almost a quarter of a century ago my brother Doug was living in a three-walled shack in the Coast Range in Oregon. If memory serves me he was taking the winter off. What exactly he was taking the winter off <u>from</u>, I don't really remember. My guess is that he was taking a break from a couple of years of wandering around the country. He used to wander around America a lot, and then park his weary feet somewhere and wander around his head for a spell.

I spent a little time doing the same, and I have to tell you that there is more danger lurking in the twisted turnpikes of my mind, than can be found on any dark highway. I don't know if I'm man enough to spend a whole winter in what I consider to be my last frontier. I'd probably start feuding with myself and one of me would wind up dead. Of course on the bright side, I'd get to go to my own funeral.

But let's go back to the shack for now. When Doug needed supplies he would travel the many miles into town using his rig of choice. His feet were not only his favorite rig, but quite often back then, they were his only choice. Doug regularly traveled more miles by foot and thumb, than I did by auto, in any given year. By not owning a car, Doug didn't have to worry about tires, insurance, or constantly checking his dipstick. (*Since I have no idea who all is reading this, I better stop right now with any references about his dipstick)*

One day Doug decided to take a longcut through the woods on a rarely traveled dirt road. He was beboppin along when all of a sudden, a hermit looking fella with a rifle, poked his head out from behind a tree, and asked Doug about his business. Doug told the old codger that when a person lives in a three-walled shack in the woods, he probably has little if any business. The old man saw no harm in that logic and invited Doug up to his place for some coffee and some talk. The old hermit's name was Glen, and I really don't remember his last name. Last names aren't a real high priority in my mental garden and first names don't always take root either.

Anyway, Doug and Glen walked quite a ways and then went up another dirt road until they got to the top. What Doug saw was a simple two-story farmhouse sitting on top of one of the larger hills around that area. The house was in good condition, but what made it unique, was that it had never been graced with plumbing or electricity.

Glen had a woodstove for heat, lanterns for light, and his choice of three natural springs to supply his water needs. About a hundred feet out his front door was his main spring, which came out of the base of a large boulder. The cool, clear water collected into a pool about the size of a birdbath. Sitting on a smaller rock was a tin cup, for drinking some of the sweetest water I have ever tasted.

I was drinking from that cup one day when I heard one hell of a racket coming from a thicket nearby. I remembered Glen speaking of bears being around so I knew what it was. And then a strange thing happened. As I tried investigating the racket, the thicket kept getting further away, and yet it wasn't moving. It took me awhile to figure out that while my mind was trying to get closer to the thicket, my feet (*acting without my permission*) were hightailing it back to the Glen's house. (*Which kind of proves that my feet are a whole lot smarter than the rest of me, and I have mixed emotions about that.*)

Glen had a handful of abandoned cars scattered around the yard's natural landscape. These ancient cars would fetch a pretty penny these days except that during those days, Glen had been using them as chicken coops. His chickens had the luxury of nesting in some really fine automobiles from the thirties and forties. Glen collected their treasured eggs each day. He ate a lot of them and the excess he would haul into town periodically to barter for groceries.

Glen had nowhere to plug in the refrigerator that was never there, but he had a closet on his back porch that was lined in burlap. Throughout the day he would open the door to this closet and splash some spring or rainwater on the burlap. The evaporation process inside this closet kept his perishables fairly cool. Of course we can't tell the state health inspectors about this refrigeration technique or they would shut Glen down for his own protection. Even though Glen had successfully spent the last seventy years living life without their protection. Think about this last paragraph for a minute.

One day, Glen and Doug were talking at his kitchen table for a long spell. As suppertime approached he asked Doug if he liked fried chicken. Doug nodded yes and then watched as the old hermit pulled a rifle off the wall, slid open his kitchen window and shot one or two of the nearby chickens in the head. Glen did all of this without ever leaving his chair. While Doug did the plucking and the cleaning, Glen fired up his wood cookstove and got busy preparing the rest of the dinner. As the sun went down, they ate until they couldn't anymore and then continued talking deep into the night.

Doug took to visiting Glen quite a bit. They both had a lot of stories to exchange, and each genuinely appreciated the others simple, yet honest approach to life. Even when Doug's thumb would take him away to points unknown, whenever he wandered close to that stretch of the Coast Range, Doug would make the long trek to visit with his friend. When Doug went to visit he always brought along some salt, beans, coffee, flour, and a great big tin of Top tobacco, which always pleased the old man.

Doug was a hermit of the highway, while Glen was a hermit of the hills. One drank up life all over this country, while one spent his entire life drinking out of three springs.

Many decades have passed since then. If Glen is still alive, he's pushing a hundred. And if he is still breathing, I know that he's still breathing the air on top of his mountain. He told me once that he would stay there until he died.

Doug's thumb finally led him to ten acres of his own dirt up in Alaska. His first ten years up north were spent with no electricity or plumbing. You learn to adjust I guess. He told me a few years ago that he finally got not only plumbing and electricity, but a phone as well. He also said that for the first time in his life he had to go to the bank and get one of those things called a checking account. Doug was forty something and finally had what the rest of us refer to as "*bills*." I told him it sounded to me like he was turning into a yuppie bastard and getting kind of soft in his old age.

I've only seen Doug twice in the last fourteen years, but I hear from him every year or three. I've thought about paying him a surprise visit, but I tried that once twenty years ago when he was living in a shack in Colorado. Even back then he was living without plumbing or electricity and wintering on beans, biscuits and moonstruck venison. He caught wind of my intended arrival and rode the wind to Arkansas for a couple of months. He'd never been on an Arkansas joyride before so I don't blame him for heading out. I finally caught up with him a year or two later. I can't remember where or why. We tend to weave in and out of each other's lives every few years. These occasions are always fun and special, although we both usually wind up with a severe headache the next day. Go figure.

I should call Doug to find out if he's dead or not, but while he does own a phone these day's, he very rarely answers it. Yuppie hermit bastard.

Thit!

It was a casual gathering. Just myself, two thirds of my boys, my ex-brother in law, his wife and their two young sons, my ex-wife and her fiancé, and one fourth of the sons of a girl I use to date, who coincidentally happened to be the ex-wife of my ex-wife's fiancé? OK, so it was a bit of a confusing gathering but it was indeed casual.

The evening was proceeding fairly uneventful until a bowl of pistachios was placed in front of me. Now I have spent my entire life knowing that on any given day, any common object poses a threat to my person. I have been KO'd (*Knocked Out*) by a eighty pound case of pork before, (*long story, not pretty, don't want to talk about it.*) I was once KG'd (*Knocked Goofy*) by a gas-powered weedeater falling 12 feet and striking me on the head, (*shorter story, again not pretty, don't want to talk about it either.*) And believe it or not I was even the recipient of a full airborne attack by two 12-pound turkeys one time. I wasn't angered by their assault on my head. It was the fact that they were frozen solid at the time, which hurt the most.

Anyway, on this particular night, we had all gathered around the kitchen table to play a board game. By habit, I scan the room for any obvious implements of death that I may need to be wary of. There is nothing but pistachios and my ex-wife's car keys in front of me. Her fiancé grabs the keys and very cleverly hangs them on the corner of a post behind me. My ex-wife comments to her fiancé that I will accidentally knock them off during the game. Sure enough, a half an hour into the game I lean back in my chair and accidentally knock them off. She laughs and says, "*I told you so*" to her fiancé. I pick up the keys and think to myself

"At least I didn't get hurt, although the night is still young."
I scan the room once more for any danger that may be lurking.

During the game we all nibbled on the pistachios. The problem with pistachios is that not all of them have that convenient crack in their armor, allowing you entrance to the meat. Since I didn't have a nutcracker handy, I popped one of those closed nuts into my mouth and very carefully started to crush it's shell between my teeth.

What happened next was both painful, perplexing, and a personal first. As I bit down on the nut, the shell opened up wide enough to firmly bite my tongue. Naturally I screamed and everyone turned to see what my problem was.

I shouted "***Thit, Thit, Thit, it'th tuck on my tongue, it'th tuck on my tongue and it hurth***!"

Ath I wath telling them thith, my tongue wath thooting in and out of my mouth with the pithathio thtill firmly biting it. I looked like a thtarving anteater at an all you can eat buffet. All of thith happened while we were in a routhing game of Trivial Purthoot, which coenthadently, I wath loothing at the time. After a minute or two of eye watering terror, I manage to remove the nut from the death grip it had on my tongue. I don't know why I'm thtill talking thith way, the bleeding thtopped and no thurgery wath nethathary.

I'm not thure why I'm curthed with theeth kind of thtrange accthidenth. I know that thit happenth. I jutht don't know why thit happenth to me tho mutth. Who could have guethed that a thimple pithatheo could be tho dangerouth. Ith nothing thacred anymore?

The Airport

In the mid 1970's, I was handed the opportunity to catch a much needed free ride in a very small three-seater airplane. Just for your information, a three-holer outhouse is like sitting in the lap of luxury compared to spending fourteen hours in a three-seater airplane. Anyway, this flight was to depart from the airport where I spent a great deal of my youth. It turned out to be the first leg of a hitchhiking journey that would take me from my home in Oregon, to that famous mile high city in Colorado, with Illinois in mind as my eventual destination.

I was in the first stages of a troubled marriage and had been contemplating a journey by thumb to visit an old friend in the windy city of Chicago. A buddy of mine who knew of my dilemma, called one evening and asked how much myself and my backpack weighed. I told him that while this was a very personal question, I was naturally curious as to why he asked. He went on to inform me that his dad was flying a little puddle jumper to Denver in four days and had room for an additional five hundred pounds of freight. Since I had traveled as cargo before, I was naturally ready to jump at the chance to do it again.

I told Chuck that I weighed about a hundred and sixty pounds and my fully loaded backpack was another ninety five. He said that if I could lose fifteen pounds in four days, we could both hitch a plane ride to Colorado, and from there head to points unknown. I have always liked heading to points unknown (especially without the cumbersome restraints of a job) so I quit my lucrative position of dishwasher at the Hereford Steer Restaurant, commenced packing and four days later showed up at the Corvallis Airport at the crack of dawn.

I have mixed emotions about using a capital **A** when speaking of the Corvallis **A**irport since it was such a small and insignificant place. Prior to the last twenty years, Corvallis was just another small town with a county renowned cow college and an airport that wasn't renowned for much of anything. I'm not sluicing ducks, I'm just telling you how it used to be.

Upon my arrival at the airport, Chuck's dad hefted my pack to take an approximate guess on its weight. A few years earlier I had carried that same backpack coast to coast, and through much trial and error, knew which items could be left out to make it lighter. The heaviest item I left behind on this trip was my cast iron skillet.

Out of the 26 states I had hitchhiked through a few years earlier, I had used the skillet only a few times during a ten-day stint at Edisto Beach in South Carolina. I liked having it around because a cast iron skillet is handy not only for cooking, but for self-defense should push come to shove. And believe it or don't, push do come to shove occasionally while your on the road.

Chuck's dad threw our gear into his plane and then threw out some of <u>his</u> things to lighten the load. The two items that I remember the most were his pistol and a fire extinguisher. I was a little uneasy about flying without a weapon (*First no skillet, and now no pistol*) but I was real nervous about leaving the fire extinguisher behind. After all, like I used to tell my folks during my childhood, **"Sometimes fire just happens."**   And it really just does.... **sometimes.**

As we took off down the runway and up into the sky I couldn't help but look down at the tiny airport where I had spent so much of my youth. It brought back a lot of memories of simpler, pre-marital days.

My brothers and I spent a lot of time at that airport for many reasons. One reason being that we lived out in the country and while the thought of a cold pop and a candy bar on a hot summer day always sounded good, it required an awful lot of bike pedaling to get to the nearest store. Fortunately for us, the airport was only about a mile from our house and had not only a cold pop machine but a candy machine as well.

The pop machine was a bit of a disappointment as it only sold Fanta sodas. I despised most of the Fanta flavors, but my rural, pre-teen, refined pallet could tolerate their version of grape soda. On a hot summer day it was well worth the dime it took to buy.

We didn't bother stealing the empty soda bottle for the three cent deposit, since the airport was the only place we knew that carried Fantas. As a rule, we regularly picked up all empty beer and pop bottles along the roads back then to redeem them for the cash deposit. But since no one would redeem Fantas, we usually put them out of our misery with a well-aimed rock or bullet. It's kind of a gruesome end for a pop bottle and also dangerous for us barefooters who spent a lot of time in ditches.

I cut my feet on a lot on broken ditch glass while I was young and foolish, and the odds are pretty good that I cut my feet on some of the same glass that I had dispatched with a rock or bullet at an earlier age. I guess you might call it Cola Karma. These days I find myself pretty much old and foolish, and still spending a lot of time in ditches, but I wear shoes more often and recycle at every opportunity.

The airport's candy bar machine only had a choice of about six or seven varieties but since candy is candy, a kid with a quarter is king. It was the type of machine that had pull handles on it for making your selection. I had put my money into it one day and since I was only about ten and had all the time in the world, I found myself pulling the knob out and then letting it slide back in very slowly. Most people just pulled the handle out, released it and watched as the candy dropped into the tray below. I still don't know why I pulled the handle slowly on that particular day. It's just a gift with ten-year-old boys I guess.

Anyway, I pulled the knob all the way out, and let it slide back in very slowly. About halfway to it's resting place I heard and felt (*through the knob*) a **click** and then watched as the candy fell into the tray below, making a **kerplunking** sound. Rather than turning loose of the knob and letting it finish it's journey home, for some unknown reason I pulled it back again towards me. I then let it start heading back towards the machine until it clicked again and I'll be darned if another candy bar didn't **kerplunk** into the tray.

While the candy bars were dropping I remember thinking to myself "*This is dishonest* (**Kerplunk**.) *Boy o boy this is dishonest* (**Kerplunk**.) *Oh no, I'm being dishonest again* (**Kerplunk**.) *I better stop pretty soon* (**Kerplunk**,) *because while this may be great for me* (**Kerplunk**) *it's tragic for the vending* (**Kerplunk**) *company. And just how am I supposed to sleep tonight with all this* (**Kerplunk**) *guilt, and all this* (**Kerplunk**) *candy?*"

I had hit the mother lode of chocolate. I looked left and right, scooped up all the candy and raced home to tell my brothers about my latest discovery. I explained the whole technical process and naturally they couldn't believe their ears. We all agreed that there was only one thing left to do. Our mission was clear should we decide to except it.

The next day we went back with a grocery bag and drained the whole damn machine with just under three dollars in change. Morally we knew it was wrong, but collectively we felt we had a pretty good mechanical loophole, should the legal system get involved.

Looking back on it all now, I don't think what we did was wrong. After all, there was no sign posted saying not to do what we had just done, and that seems to be all it takes in today's legal world. As a matter of fact I could probably still sue the airport for all of the cavities I got from eating all that candy. <u>Is this a great country or what!</u>

The next time the candy vendor restocked the candy machine however, he couldn't understand why the machine was bone dry, with only a handful of change in the coin holder. Naturally he talked to the guy behind the ticket counter.

The guy who worked behind the ticket counter was the spitting image of the skinny black haired costar of the old TV show, *Voyage To The Bottom Of The Sea.* I don't remember his name so let's just refer to him as *the skinny black haired guy who was the spitting image of some TV star from Voyage To The Bottom Of The Sea.*

Well that isn't gonna work. It's just too damn long. Let's just call him Ed for short. Although he wasn't short, actually he was kinda tall and skinny. **Hold it!** Wait a cotton pickin minute! I'm honing in on a name............
Richard Basehart.

HAH! You didn't think my mind worked very well anymore did you?

UH-OH, wait another minute. My mistake. Richard Basehart played the Captain of the submarine on *Voyage To The Bottom Of The Sea.* Ed (*not his real TV name*) was Richard Basehart's assistant captain, or head lieutenant or assistant manager or something. Whatever you called him, Ed was definitely the next in charge if Richard Basehart (*not his real TV name either*) died. And we all knew he wouldn't die because he was the star of the show. And actually, Ed probably wouldn't die either because he was the co-star. But I'm digressing aren't I?

Hold it! I'm honing in on another name..... **Conway Twitty?** Wait a cotton pickin minute. I don't know which section of my battered brain that came from, but I think I better belt up and lock the hubs while driving down these muddy roads. This is getting just plain spooky.

Anyway, Ed (*formerly known as the skinny black haired co-star of Voyage To The Bottom Of The Sea*) had noticed us hanging around the candy machine a few days earlier with a grocery bag, but hadn't a clue as to what was in it. Although after his discussion with Mr. Candy Vendor Man, he was starting to get a pretty good idea.

After the grocery bag incident, Ed started watching us real closely at the candy machine and everywhere else for that matter. The Vending Machine Company also fixed the machine before we had eaten our way to the bottom of the grocery bag, so our free ride on the candy caboose came to a sudden stop. It was a sad day, but a fun trip while it lasted.

My brothers and I also spent a lot of time riding bikes on the airport's runways. The runways were made of cement and the seams were heavily tarred on a regular basis. On really hot days the tar would bubble, and when you rode your bike on these seams there would be a glorious crackling sound that was quite addicting.

Now I know what you're thinking. You're thinking my brothers and I were simpletons. Not true. Boy's just lean towards having simple fun, and there is a big difference......Well OK, maybe we were simpletons, but I like to think that we were complex simpletons. **(?)**

You could also collect this soft tar until you had enough to form what can only be described as a large black tarball. Since there is virtually no use for a large black tarball, about the only thing you can really do with it is place it on your dresser when you get home. The down side to this is when the sun comes baking through your bedroom window, hits the tarball, and makes it melt down the side of the dresser. When you come home from a long, hot day of bean picking, the sight of a dresser covered in a thin layer of black road tar can be quite amusing. Quite amusing for children anyway. My parent's sense of humor was lost somewhere between the birth of demon-child number one and demon-child number five. Oddly enough they got their sense of humor back about the same time they started having grand-demons. Figure that one out.

As the years went by we progressed from bicycles to racing go-karts and motorcycles at the airport. I shot a motorcycle well past 100 MPH on one of their runways at age fourteen. The airport officials weren't always crazy about this sort of adventure so we had to hit it fast and then hightail it back home and try to look innocent. I don't know if you've ever tried to look innocent when your not, but it can be very taxing. It is almost easier to not be guilty, than to have to pretend to be innocent......... Almost

Anyway, back to my plane ride. As the tiny plane took off and circled, taking me on my way to Denver, I also noticed the two hundred-foot tall, red and white checkered watertower beside the airport. I wondered then and still wonder now if the initials I scratched into the top of it thirty years ago with my pocketknife are still there.

While I may not know whether my initials are still there, I do know that they had to replace the light bulb cover (*on the very top of the tower*) at least once. The light was there to keep planes from crashing into the tower at night. The reason I know they had to replace the bulb cover at least once is because Brother Dan climbed up and stole it one night.

After he stole the cover, Dan also unscrewed the lightbulb just enough to make it go out. I think he probably did this so that he could escape under the cover of darkness, and of course leave his fingerprints behind on the bulb. After he'd climbed down and was running from the scene of the crime however, he looked back and noticed the bulb was back on. This gave him an eerie feeling and his pace picked up accordingly.

It was exactly this sort of behavior that made the whole family realize that Dan was the one bad apple in our bunch. My brothers and I may have stolen one (or a dozen) of the many pretty blue lightbulb covers that lined the runway for night landings, after all there were lot's of those. But there was only one watertower light bulb keeping planes from crashing into it. **Bad Dan! Bad Dan**!

All told it was a good airport for my brothers and I. Unfortunately the officials never felt my brothers and I were all that good for the airport. Go figure.

On retrospect, I think it was pretty much all Dan's fault.

THE FALL OF MAN

My first big fall in this strange odyssey I call *life*, occurred at about age three. My folks were rebuilding a house, which had cement stairs leading up to the front door landing and my dad hadn't installed a porch rail yet. Since the porch that I had wandered out onto was twice as tall as I was, you can only imagine the surprise and terror I felt, when a large gust of wind came along blowing me clean off the porch and head first into the driveway. Looking back on it now, that not only explains many of the potholes in my parent's driveway but some of the ones on my head as well.

After a while you get use to falling off things while attempting to survive childhood. You're never real happy about them, but while they are unexpected, they are also so frequent that you become jaded to them. I went from having thoughts like (***Oh my god I'm not only falling but plumetting to my death as well!***) to having thoughts like (*Oh great, I'm falling again, this is gonna hurt. I'll just bet it's a bonebreaker, Yep, it was.*)

My next big fall came when I attempted to jump from our stove oil tank to a clothesline. I miscalculated and didn't take into account the laws of centrifugal force. (*Cut me some slack, I was only five!*) I was forcefully pulled off the clothesline, landed with my arm behind my back and naturally broke my arm.

Because of the weight of a *fingertip to shoulder* cast my falling off of things not only accelerated but also continued well beyond the removal of the cast. Falling not only continued well beyond that cast and several others, but has pursued me through my teens, twenties, thirties and unfortunately my forties as well.

Falling off bicycles, motorcycles, horses, tractors, ladders, barns, sheds, chicken coops and trees became so routine that unless it required a cast or stitches you just dusted yourself off and kept on going. On occasion we'd all be sitting at the dinner table and one of my folks would say "*What a coincidence, here we are eating pork chops while one of you boy's seems to be bleeding like a stuck hog!*" At this point each one of us boys would look at ourselves and then each other, to figure out who was bleeding more profusely. It was always a clear sign that one of my parents had a bad day at work, when they just weren't in the mood for excessive bleeding at the dinner table. (*It's not easy growing up with strict parents.*)

I remember riding on the back of a motorcycle that kid brother Dan was piloting one day. We were both about a dozen years old and heading from one section of the farm to the next. (*Doesn't it strike you just a little odd that my kid brother and I were both about a dozen years old?*) Anyway we were zipping along at a fairly healthy clip since under normal circumstances a dirt road is a fairly smooth riding surface and perfect for zipping along at a fairly healthy clip. Especially when you have made so many trips down that road that every pothole, rock, road-kill, tree root and washout is as familiar as the back of your scarred up hand.

On this particular day however, what we hadn't counted on was that the farmer had been plowing the fields on both sides of the road and for a couple of passes forgot to pick up the plow to prevent digging up the road as well. Dan and I hit the plowed section of the road at about thirty-mph.

Since Dan had the handlebars to hold onto, he didn't fall off, even though his butt was slapping the seat like an atomic cookie cutter. I however, was a passenger with nothing to hold onto but Dan's waist, and the main reason I fell off was because I wasn't holding onto his waist. Even at an early age of twelve, boys realize that holding onto another males waist is just something they aren't comfortable with. Although if I would have had a death grip on Dan's waist, I probably wouldn't have fallen off the motorcycle. Or I would have fallen off, but also drug Dan along with me. I wish that had happened instead, but alas it didn't.

As I was falling off the motorcycle I noticed that everything was happening in slow motion. I fell off in slow motion, I bounced and rolled in slow motion, I screamed in slow motion, and Dan's motorcycle taillight disappeared into a cloud of dust in slow motion.

After a bit, Dan pulled his motorcycle over and took inventory of the situation. He knew that the last time he had seen me I was sitting right behind him and now I seemed to be missing. Dan also noticed the mushroom cloud of dust on the dirt road behind him. He figured I was probably at the center of the dust cloud (*Well, Duh*). He also figured I was probably mad as a wet hen (*Well, Double Duh*). But since Dan was fearless even as a child, he rode on back to face the music.

Since I was wearing nothing but cut-offs, I was a dustier shade of pale when he found me. I wanted to yell at him but I needed to spit about a cup of dirt and rocks out of my mouth first. I was also concerned about the blood that was coming out of my toes. Dust and blood turn into mysterious mud that is kind of disturbing.

I lost two or three toenails, and various other remnants of hide during that fall. I never did find them, and that's the worst of it all. As if it isn't bad enough how embarrassing falling is, quite often you also lose things in the process.

I fell off of a truck once, lost a whole fingernail, and never did find it. *By the way, there are those that would have you believe it was a turnip truck that I fell off of but this is untrue.*

I fell off a tractor once, lost a strip of hide from my arm, and never got it back. I fell off of my icy roof once, lost a days pay, and never got it back. I fell in love once, lost my virginity, never got it back either but I've been single so long that I think I may be gaining ground. That's kind of a good news bad news thing.

I've fallen in love a few times since and lose a little piece of my heart each time I do. I can't really tell if I get any of that back or not, but I'm hoping so. These are probably the hardest falls of all, but I still pick myself up, dust myself off and keep on falling anyway.

KITTY

I have an aunt Kitty. I also have an Aunt Rosie, but this isn't a story about either one of them. Although truth be known, Rosie could not only take Kitty in a fair fight, but would probably have also had her planted in the ground before the dust had even settled.

But this isn't a story about catfights amongst my clan. Anyway I don't think it is. I never know where my stories are heading, but my intent this time is to write about cats.

But you know, it would be one hell of a catfight between Kitty (who married a college all-star) and Rosie (who married a cowboy who didn't have much of anything.)

As long as we're on the subject of my Aunt Rosie, I remember walking with her and my mom one day. We were heading from Rosie's house to her barn, which was quite away's away. We were walking along and Rosie was talking about how much she loved Elvis. I was young enough that this struck me as odd that she was in love with someone called Elvis, while she was married to someone I called Uncle Don. I planned to tell Uncle Don about this newly acquired information but when we got down to the barn, Don and my dad were preparing for surgery on a cow that was down on it's side. The cow was dead and so I put the Elvis bomb on the back burner.

I remember it's belly being so bloated that it caused the uphill legs to point at about a forty five degree angle. (*I'm referring to the cow here, not Elvis. Although in his later years...... oh never mind, let's let them both rest in peace*) Anyway, I didn't know much as a small boy, particularly about the effects of Elvis on married women, but I did know that bloaters are usually not eaters, no matter how hungry you think you are. As far as I knew the cow had just up and died and the adults were going to dispose of it somehow. I paid extremely close attention, because messing around with dead things just intrigues the hell out of small boys and in all honesty, I accelled at being a small boy. Truth be known, I still do.

I remember my dad and my Uncle Don standing around the carcass with a hand saw an ax and some knives. I figured they were going to quarter and bury the carcass. *Carcass. What a classy sound for something that really isn't. God, I love that word. That doesn't make me a bad person does it? Never mind, don't answer, I was just typing out loud for a moment. I might not let it happen again....... I might not.*

Anyway, the conversation between my dad and my Uncle Don went something like this:

" *Boy it's really bloated ain't it?*"

" *Yep.*"

" *Well, I guess one of us had better pop it.*"

" *Yep.*"

" *You wanna do it?*"

" *Nope.*"

" *Are you sure?*"

" *Yep.*"

" *All right then stand back, I'm going in.*"

" *Go right ahead.*"

" *I think I'm gonna cut it's belly right about.... here.*"

" *Good Idea, I think I'll stand way over....................................... here.*"

" *Look at how fast the legs drop when you pop it's belly, and god oh mighty that's one hell of a smell ain't it.*"

" *Yep, and thank god I was standing way over....................................... here.*"

" *Well I guess I'll continue cutting right about.... here.*"
" *Careful now, if you accidentally cut that thing right there and it gets on the meat, it'll taint it so bad it'll ruin it for eating.*"

As the organs and blood started flying, the words "***It'll ruin it for eating***" kept echoing in my little head, and then all of a sudden I realized that this bloated batch of bovine botulism was heading towards our bellies instead of a hole in the pasture where it smelled like it belonged. This whole episode turned my stomach for about four seconds until my carnivorous instincts kicked in and I suddenly found myself hungry enough to kill for a hamburger.

Small boy's are like that, and actually so are big boy's, which makes me wonder if the cow had really up and died, or if Don and my dad had just wanted a burger real bad.

I also wondered if Don would be able to finish that succulent burger, when I dropped the bomb about Rosie and Elvis.

CATS

Notes to myself:
What a great title for a musical.
Must remember to talk to Andrew Lloyd Webber.
 Must also try to remember to remove notes to myself from story.

I honestly attempted to write about cats in my previous story, titled ***Kitty***, but as is often the case, my mind took a fork in the road and I wound up in a barn with my Aunt Rosie, a bloated cow, and Elvis. I would apologize, but by now you have probably realized that I have little control over my mind or the direction of my stories. In my defense however, you must understand that over the last forty years my head has received more direct hits than the Bismarck and the toll has been fairly obvious. This time however, I am going to try really hard to stay on track. I was a sprinter in track, although my favorite event was high jumping. (*OOPS, I just did it again didn't I? Do you see how hard it is?*)

Anyway, I have always had mixed emotions about cats. If you divide the world into two groups, you will find that there are Cat people and then there are dog people. The reason I use a capitol letter in Cat and not in dog, is because I firmly believe that is how Cats would prefer it.

Cats are self-assured, and in charge of their domain, much like a beautiful woman on a tropical beach, with the wind blowing through her hair. The prettier the girl, the more of the beach is her domain. A cat is positive that its domain is the whole damn beach.

Dogs on the other hand usually spend their time on the beach in the shade, where they are usually happy or tired or both and either way they are perpetually plagued by gas, which is not unlike most all males if you really think about it. This raises a question. When a dog smells a really foul odor, does he blame it on the dog, or does he point his paw at the humans in the room? Oh sure, **you** might not care about the answer, but I've been known to lose a lot of sleep over less important questions. Maybe my boy's are right, maybe I do need to get out more.

Anyway, I have always been a dog person, until a handful of years ago, when I found myself the proud owner of a fairly average cat that did fairly average cat type things. It wasn't much trouble, so I made the adjustment fairly smoothly. Fairly smoothly that is until one cold winter morning when I discovered just how ferocious a feline can be.

I had woken up at 6:00 a.m. and was making a beeline to my cherished coffeepot. Back in those days I used to sleep buck naked, but since I really didn't like cruising around the house that way, I would throw my bathrobe on. While I was putting it on, I noticed how cold my upstairs bedroom was. I remembered the heat being on downstairs when I went to bed the night before, so I started speculating as to why it was now as cold as an icebox.

I knew that on occasion my boys liked turning the heat up in their room until it was hot enough to forge metal. Fortunately when they would do this, the heater's internal fuse would blow thus disabling the heater until the reset button is pushed. Unfortunately those of us who slept upstairs, depended on this heater as well.

In order to reset the heater in my boy's room I had to do the following: 1) Find a long, skinny piece of metal that would fit through the heater grate to reach the reset button. 2) Get down on my hands and knees. 3) Push the skinny piece of metal through the grate and hope that I would hit the reset button and not a coil, or hunk of wire that would give me an unexpected permanent, or send me to an early grave.

So there I was, blue from the cold, buck naked except for my bathrobe, not an ounce of caffeine in my system, and as if all of that weren't enough (and don't you really think it should've been) I'm also terrified of electricity. Terrified for good reason I might add. I ran into a lot of electric fence when I was growing up and learned to hate those occasions. Granted, I never learned to hate those occasions enough to stop running into the damn fences, but I still hated those occasions none the less.

So anyway, there I am, on hands and knees, buck naked except for my bathrobe and nervously poking a metal object into a live electric wall heater, with nothing more than a match to guide me in the darkness. Not a particularly smart thing to do, but I've never implied that I was employed by NASA.

While I was in the middle of this endeavor, unbeknownst to me, our cat had crawled into the southern entrance of my bathrobe, apparently saw something threatening, and with one mighty swing of it's paw, tried to destroy and kill what I can only assume he thought to be a really weird looking canary. (?)

Since I knew we didn't own a canary, much less keep one in my bathrobe, I naturally screamed. No, that's a lie, I actually screamed quite unnaturally. There was after all nothing natural about a cat going bird hunting at six a.m. in my bathrobe. Weird looking canary or not, even in my own twisted mind, this cat was just plain out of line. There ain't no way man's best friend would've done something like that.

PICKIN & GRINNIN

I spent more than a dozen summers of my youth planting and picking crops out in the fields, and at the time naturally despised it. Well, actually, since I hit the fields at a very early age, I should say that I *learned* to despise it. When you're planting and picking at age four or five, you're not really sharp enough to hate what you're doing. The average four or five year old is pretty much just short and hungry, regardless of whether he is at home or in a beanfield. I was no exception, other than the fact that I was exceptionally short and hungry.

We planted and picked, strawberries, raspberries, blueberries, beets, corn, apples, pears, peaches, pumpkins, nuts, beans, bark and even pine cones. If it grew in the Willamette Valley, we picked and or planted it, and we didn't restrict ourselves to just produce either. As normal (?) bloodthirsty boys, we also dabbled in picking and planting small critters, but those were lousy experiments with minimal yields and I've since been advised not to discuss it any further without legal council present.

Of the many downsides to spending your little life picking produce, one is in the actual picking technique. With strawberries, you pretty much have just two choices. You either crawl around on your hands and knees in the soft wet soil or you spend all day, bent over, with straight legs. Having spent a decade doing both, I can honestly say that both equally suck. That may sound rather harsh but it's the truth. There is nothing glamorous about stoop labor.

When you spend all day on your knees in the mud, you have to be certain you're earning enough quarters to cover the price of replacing your three-dollar jeans. You not only blow the knees out of your pants toot sweet, but you also realize by the end of the day, that these trousers will never see a washing machine again.

Mud starched pants are not only a pain to take off but worse yet to put back on come the following morning. If you are lucky enough for the mud to have dried, the pants are so stiff that they will stand up on their own. At this point it is best to take them outside and beat the hell out of them against a slow moving dog or kid brother, depending on which is the least dangerous.

If the mud on your pants is still wet, they are fairly easy to put on, but trust me, at five a.m. you really don't want to. They are not only wet and cold but also your big toe hangs up in the hole in the knee, nine times out of ten. Their is virtually no benefit to beating the hell out of wet, muddy pants against a slow moving dog or kid brother other than the fact that the ensuing battle will get your heart racing faster than three pots of coffee.

When you decide to save your knees and pick berries while bent over all day, it is extremely difficult to straighten up at the end of your shift. Some days it was so difficult that I would actually find myself having to walk home backwards at the end of the day, with my head tucked between my legs, so as to see where I was going. While walking home backwards, I also realized that since I would probably never straighten up again, I was also doomed to spend the rest of my life eating off of the floor, which put me in the toxic airspace of the methane monster I referred to as, my dog.

Another down side to picking strawberries is that it is extremely difficult to get away with anything. Thanks to my mom, my siblings and I were all born with our butts too close to the ground, but in spite of how short we were, a strawberry plant offered little cover. For true mischief, a bean field was much more adventure friendly.

My mom kept a pretty tight reign on her herd while we were picking, but after a number of years, she got a job in town and her watchful eye was no longer upon us. This was a bona fide good news, bad news scenario. It was good news for her herd, but often bad news for whomever we were picking for. You just don't turn five Tasmanian devils loose and hope that all will be well by the time you get home.

I was about five when I first hit the bean field and could only pick one or two coffee cans worth of beans in a day's time. Eight or nine years later, I was picking close to three hundred pounds a day. We were paid two and a quarter cents per pound, with a quarter of a cent per pound bonus if we worked at least six days a week, which we always did.

By the time I was a teenager, three hundred pounds of beans would fetch almost seven dollars for a full day of nose to the grindstone bean picking. Pretty good money in those days when you consider that the brand new motorcycle I had my eye on was only about two hundred dollars. I never got it, but I did have my eye on it, which was the next best thing.

When we were picking strawberries, we got paid thirty-five cents per carrier. A carrier held about a dozen baskets. If the carrier wasn't full enough, you didn't get paid enough. Short of spending hours strategically stacking berries to make a three quarters full basket look like a full basket there is virtually no way to cheat while picking berries. Beans however were a different story.

It didn't take long for me to realize that the heavier the beanbag, the more I got paid. I'm not proud of it, but there were more then a few days when a few dirt clods got mixed in with the beans to help the bag weigh more. I also learned to drag my bag through any mud puddles just before weighing it. A gallon of water weighs around seven pounds. If you can get two gallons of water to hitch a ride in a bag of beans, it was an extra quarter heading to your pocket no matter how you looked at it. Naturally I also scanned the ditches on my way to the fields each day for lead tire weights.

I'll just bet I know what you're thinking. Your thinking that between the dirt clods and the water, I was basically stealing. Well that thought crossed my little mind back then also but believe it or don't, I knew the difference between weight misrepresentation and stealing.

When you're caught falsifying bean weight, you get a dirty look. When you're caught stealing beans, you get thrown out of the beanfield, which did not set well with my hard working parents. However, if you want to talk about a really severe crime, try getting caught stealing Ding-Dongs out of a bean pickers sack lunch. Hell hath no fury like a bean picker with a missing Ding-Dong.

Looking back on it now, if I'd have spent as much time picking, as I spent trying to get a fifty pound bag of beans to weigh sixty pounds, I might have owned that new motorcycle, instead of just dreaming about it.

After a number of years, small boys lose interest in picking beans and they start to look for more adventure in the field. This naturally coincided with my mom's watchful eye no longer being present. What we didn't know at the time however, was that she had handed her watchful eye over to a row boss named Naomi. I think she kept my mom's eye in her pocket. Naomi could draw that eye out of her pocket quicker than Wyatt Earp could draw his pistol. It was next to impossible to get away with anything while

Naomi was on patrol. A lot of us boys started referring to her, in hushed tones, as Naomi the Nazi.

Back in those days, a beanfield rowboss, had more power and control over us pickers then J. Edgar Hoover had over John F. Kennedy. The only difference between J. Edgar and Naomi is that I don't know that Naomi ever wore a dress. J. Edgar however.........

Anyway, during the time of Naomi's reign of terror, the biggest thing to hit the movie theaters in many years, was James Bond. For me, 007 changed my outlook on bean picking for at least a summer or two. Each day usually started with good solid intentions of picking as many beans as possible, but as the day wore on, boredom set in and the next thing you knew, Secret Agent Activities would find their way into our busy schedules.

As Secret Agents our missions were clear, should we decide to accept them, and we always excepted them. We would blow up dams (*overhead irrigation pipe*) with plastic explosives (*a mudball with a bean poking out of it for a fuse*). We would detonate the explosives by strategically lobbing grenades (*dirt clods)* at them. We regularly infiltrated enemy lines (*another pickers row*) to steal top secret microchips (*microchips of the potato variety)* from their heavily guarded vaults (*brown paper lunch sacks wrapped up inside their coats and hidden at the base of the bean plants.*)

Once these missions were accomplished the only thing left to do was to blow up enemy headquarters (*the beanfield outhouse*) with laser guided missiles (*once again using dirt clods since we were on a tight military budget.*) The enemy usually rushed out of their headquarters (*the outhouse*) confused and disorientated (*pants around ankles*) and naturally surrendered (*cursed and shook most of their fist*) to the army of Secret Agents (*small boys hiding in the oak grove*) who had outwitted and captured them. (*I hesitate using the word* **outwitted** *since a battle of wits between a band of boys in a beanfield is a very short battle at best.*)

The only times that our missions were unsuccessful were when an enemy agent of the angelic persuasion (*a female bean picker*) would walk into enemy headquarters (*same old outhouse.*) At that point the secret agent appears to have been shot by a tranquilizer dart, because his mind gets very fuzzy and just sort of wanders. His mind wanders to flowery meadows filled with bunnies and hearts, and other mushy things, until the secret agent is kind of confused, but calm and at piece with the world. At piece that is, until Naomi would once again show up.

BEANS

As I have mentioned before, my siblings and I pretty much grew up picking in the fields. We picked primarily strawberries and beans and each day started out pretty much the same. We would wake up at an inhumane hour, get driven to the field, grab a five gallon metal bucket, a cotton bean sack and head to an assigned row alongside several hundred other disgruntled and sleepy pickers. Our one common thread being that elusive two-dollar bill we earned for every hundred pounds of beans we picked.

Picking produce is tedious and boring work at best, but on occasion the monotony would be broken when you were lucky enough to pick within earshot of someone else's radio. That was always a treat since it put you in touch with the outside world so to speak. Listening to the Beatles made you feel better about being stuck in Strawberry Fields Forever and Paul Harvey's noon time commentary gave your little mind some food for thought while you ate your warm bologna sandwich with your muddy little fingers.

Stealing goodies out of other peoples lunches made one out of the two people involved happy, which I felt was better than both parties being upset. In my defense I would like to say that while I had ample opportunity to steal their whole dang lunch, I always settled for just the dessert. It would take a heartless man to take the whole meal, and I like to think that as a child I was a considerate thief. Plus why on earth would I want twice as many warm bologna sandwiches as I already had?

Every season there were tales of people finding things while picking. These rumored treasures ranged from cash, jewelry, watches, wallets, purses, pocketknives, radios and even girlie magazines. I never found any of those items but god knows I looked. And looked. And looked.

After a while the status monster would rear its ugly head, which was kind of odd since there are very few things to be proud owners of in a bean field. Cars were out of the question because while we all knew how to drive, none of us had a license to drive the car we didn't own. I couldn't even spell BMW, much less worry about buying one.

Clothes were out of the question since after the first hour, everybody wore the same disgruntled, muddy, bean picker look. Calvin Klein came out to the bean field once, threw his hands up in disgust, and claimed there was absolutely nothing he could do for any of us. That kind of beat the hell out of our self-esteem, but we kept on picking anyway.

Having your own portable transistor radio would have been something to be proud of but it was a rare day that you owned one and a rarer day that you could afford batteries for it. About the only thing left to be proud of was your bean bucket.

The five-gallon metal buckets we picked into had the boots put to them on a regular basis and consequently only had a life expectancy of one or two seasons. Periodically however, a small pile of brand new ones would show up in the field, and were snatched up on a first come, first snatch basis. Two hundred pickers fighting over two dozen buckets is not a pretty sight.

I was lucky enough to get one once and naturally guarded it with my life. It was not only new and shiny but it was a six or seven gallon bucket as well. The extra holding capacity meant for a lot less trips back to your beanbag to dump it. Since the owners discouraged taking your buckets home with you each day we had to hide them in the blackberry brambles or down by the slough depending on which end of the field we were picking.

Eventually all good things come to an end and your shiny new bucket is either stolen or eventually turns into another run of the mill old bucket, because of all of the use and abuse it is put through. A bucket is not just handy for picking and hauling beans. They are great to sit or stand on, kind of fun to throw great distances, and they make amazing sounds when you beat them against beanpoles, tractor tires or an unsuspecting but well deserving kid brother.

On really cold mornings we would gather any trash and kindling size wood we could find and build fires in our buckets to warm our little hands. Once our little hands were warm we would put a damp beanbag over the smoldering bucket, then sit on it, so we could also warm our little butts. Little butts get real cold when they're so close to the ground.

After a number of years I realized that bean picking was a dead end job. Now granted, it took me seven or eight years to figure it out, but figure it out I did, and I commenced looking around at some of the other positions.

Bean field owner was out of the question because lets face it, I didn't own one. That took me six or seven years to figure out as well. Row boss was out because I was just too darn young and Naomi the Nazi row boss, hadn't died or mysteriously disappeared yet, but we were working on both. Ticket puncher was out because they always seemed to give it to a woman with a big flowery hat that she tied on under her big chin with a big colorful ribbon. There just wasn't any way this boy was gonna wear a big flowery hat tied on under his chin with a ribbon. Just because Calvin Klein had abandoned us, didn't mean I wasn't concerned with my appearance.

That pretty much left being a *Bean Boy*. A bean boy was the most admired position in the field. All you had to do was lift the sacks onto the scales, call out the weight to the ticket puncher with the flowery hat, and then dump the beans into the 5ft.X 5ft. X 5ft. bin that was sitting on big wooden skids. Once the bin was full you hooked a tractor up to it and drug it off. The beauty of being a bean boy was you got paid about 65 cents an hour and as if that wasn't enough reason right there, you also had girls swooning all over you. I was rapidly approaching an age where I'd have been willing to pay the farmer to let me be a bean boy.

My older brothers had climbed out of the ranks to become bean boys and it amazed me the attention that the girls gave them. Most male pickers would turn in a bag of beans only when it was full. I watched an awful lot of girls pick a bucket of beans, dump it into a sack, and hurry on up to the scales. Once there, they'd commence giggling and smiling and batting their eyes, as they waited in line to get their beans weighed. Their bag of beans being no bigger than a purse.

The bean boy stood at the scale with his sun bleached wind swept hair and well-tanned muscles rippling in the sun. He was so good that even on cloudy days his muscles rippled in the sun. It's no wonder the girls were falling all over this farming version of Fabio.

I wanted his job and more importantly his fringe benefits. All I had to do was figure out how to make muscles I didn't have, ripple in the sun that wasn't always there.

NANOOK

During the early to mid 1970's, I talked a buddy of mine into hitting the road with me, on a trail heading in any direction. I had discovered early in life that heading somewhere is fun, but heading anywhere is even better. The difference being that you generally know where somewhere is. Anywhere, on the other hand, is the rest of the world.

Bob and I decided to travel by car, as opposed to by thumb, since I felt hitchhiking was generally better suited for solo traveling.

Wait a minute that isn't exactly true. I once hitchhiked with a person of the female persuasion, that I had met in Washington DC a year or two earlier, and we didn't have much trouble getting rides. As a matter of fact we rode our thumbs from New Britain, Connecticut to Farmington, New Mexico in just seven rides. This was also traveling with her dog, *Tonika Etono Wonton*. Isn't it odd that after a quarter of a century I can remember the dogs name but I really don't know if I ever knew the girls last name. Life was certainly different back in those days.

But anyway, it is still easier for a male and female and a dog to catch a ride than for two males traveling together.

Well dang it that isn't always true either. I hitchhiked with a guy named Chuck once and we didn't have much trouble getting rides all through Colorado and Nebraska. Of course the quality of the rides weren't the caliber that I had experienced coming from Connecticut, but they still got us down the road, although there were a number of close calls.

One close call in particular came when we got a ride from a one eyed veteran and his M-16 rifle that he'd smuggled back from Vietnam. Since there is more to that part of the story than I feel comfortable putting in print, we'll just let that dog lie for now.

Another close call came when Chuck and myself wound up in some dusty Colorado or Nebraska town and we somehow got separated from our back packs. About all that I remember of that incident was napping on an unfamiliar trailer house floor until our packs did indeed eventually return in the back of an El Camino. To this day I still don't remember who picked us up, what town we were in, or how the hell we eventually wound up on some new freeway heading who knows where. I do know that my original destination was Chicago, but since we never made it to Illinois, I figure we must have gotten sidetracked somewhere along the way.

Now that I think about traveling in pairs, Brother Doug and I had our thumbs on cruise control one spring several years earlier. We were heading from New Mexico to Oregon, and we were having one heck of a time getting a ride through Utah. This struck me as odd because Doug was normally very good at catching rides. Of course, it was Utah that we were trying to hitchhike through, which is fairly self-explanatory if you think about it. Seriously, just think about it for a minute.

And as long as were on the subject, I can remember traveling solo once and not being able to *buy* a ride out of Florida. I had hitchhiked into West Palm Beach and was hitting all the horse stables in search of a girl by the name of Janet Christrup, whom I'd never met, but had been told was the perfect girl for me. I never did find her so I eventually left Florida. Once again, it strikes me as odd that twenty-five years later, I can remember the name of a girl I never met, but not the name of a girl I hitchhiked halfway across the continent with. There is every possibility that a therapist would need counseling if he ever got too close a look behind these eyes.

Another hitchhiking drought happened to me one spring in Idaho. Of course part of the problem stemmed from the fact that I was holding a sign that indicated that I was heading for Oregon, while my body was standing on a freeway heading towards New York. On retrospect I wonder if maybe it wasn't just **me** that people didn't want to pick up. Which is also probably why I convinced Bob into traveling with me by car instead of by thumb.

Well isn't this odd. I've done all this typing and you've done all this reading and we're right back to where we were in the second sentence of this story. But that's what makes life very similar to hitting the road. Your intended destination isn't near as interesting, as the route you take getting there.

So anyway, Bob and I went to the big city to look for a car for our upcoming expedition. We only had a couple of hundred bucks between us so our choices were somewhat limited. After a half a day of browsing we stumbled onto a lot called *500 Motors*. I thought it was an interesting choice for a name since it not only *didn't* have *500* cars but it was very doubtful that all of their cars even had *motors*. On that lot however, we did spot a likely road warrior in the form of a baby blue, 1959 Volvo with just under 246 **billion** miles on the odometer. The dealer couldn't really swear that it was a one-owner vehicle, but Bob and I had our suspicions.

We took it for a test drive and then Bob put it through a series of rigorous tests with all the mechanical gadgets he'd brought with him. Bob has always liked his mechanical gadgets and I always trusted his mechanical instincts, which was fortunate because neither one of us really trusted mine.

Bob asked me what I thought of the car, and I told him

that if we were in a pinch, should we be misfortunate enough to have it break down on the road, we could always eat what was left of the leather seats if push should come to shove. Bob looked at me as if I was half stupid. This kind of offended me because I've never been half anything my whole life, and Bob was well aware of that fact.

Bob turned his attentions away from me and towards the car salesman. I knew how shrewd Bob was when it came to car dealers so I just made myself comfortable and waited for the financial tennis match to begin. Bob made his first offer at just a little more than half of the car's selling price of $500. I felt this was an incredibly bold move on Bob's part. It is one thing to start off the bidding with an offer of ten or twenty percent less, but Bob had jumped right into the fifty- percent bracket. The car dealer hesitated for a millisecond and then shouted "*SOLD*!" as Bob kicked himself for not offering a whole lot less.

I told Bob that it is not only hard to dicker with a man that's in a big hurry to sell, but it is often not a good sign. Bob gave me another odd look as we paid the man in cash and headed for home.

It was a hot day and halfway home we decided to go for a swim. I pulled into a rest area alongside the Willamette River, parked the car and tried to roll up the window so we could lock up all of Bob's mechanical gadgets. It was at that point that we realized that while we had put the car through some very rigorous tests, we had made a mistake in assuming that the driver's side window that was rolled *down* during the test drive could be rolled *up* if a person wanted to. And what a coincidence, there we were wanting to!

We took a look inside the door and figured out right away what the problem was. Believe it or not, the problem wasn't that there was no window. The problem was that the window was a pile of busted glass in the bottom of the door. Bob asked me what I thought we should do. I told him that we pulled over to go swimmin, so swimmin we should go. I figured we had plenty of time to think about fixing the window before our upcoming expedition.

After we got home we started getting the car ready for our big journey. We tuned it up, replaced all the belts and hoses, and washed and waxed it until it shined inside and out like a million bucks. Well actually it shined like about 300 bucks, but we were proud of it none the less. The only thing left to do was to name it.

We agreed on a name and then had our friend Jill paint it on the car. On each front fender, in blood red paint, she very professionally wrote **NANOOK**, while on the trunk she painted the words:

NANOOK
RUBS
IT

Nanook of the North was a character from a Frank Zappa song. If I remember correctly, Nanook was an Eskimo who not only rubbed it, but also cautioned people about eating yellow snow.

Having grown up in the country with two twisted older brothers, I was already painfully familiar with the hazards of eating yellow snow. I didn't need Frank's advice on that one but I couldn't help but wonder what Nanook had been rubbing.

Bob and I loaded our gear and pulled out one morning with Nanook's nose pointing northeast. After many days and many miles on many new roads, we found ourselves cruising through the Grand Tetons on an extremely cold, wet night, wishing we had remembered to replace that window.

SAM'S CAMP

I grew up on only two acres in the country, but fortunately behind our place was a farm, one or two thousand acres in size. My brothers, sister and myself spent a great deal of time working, playing, hunting, fishing, swimming and in general, growing up on that farm.

The east side of the farm was bordered by the Long Tom River. On that river was a spot that became one of our favorite swimming holes. One of the farmer's nine sons, named Sam, had his eye on my older sister and naturally he enjoyed Linda bringing her four little brothers down to that spot for our regular swims.

Before there was a road on that side of the farm, we had to park on a dike about a quarter mile away and then walk to the swimming hole. I can still remember walking barefoot across those fields and asking my mom why God put plants with stickers on the earth. I don't remember what her response was, as she patiently pulled stickers out of my squirming little foot, but to this day, I still don't see the benefit of plants with stickers.

Over the years a road was cut into that section where the farm met the river and we frequented that spot on what seemed like a daily basis. The river was perfect for swimming and fishing, and was also flanked on both sides by gravel bars, which made for wonderful rock hunting. I had a habit of breaking my arms during swimming season, so rock hunting became a very important, alternative pastime for me since casts and water are natural enemies.

One summer day, Sam brought down a backhoe to the swimming hole and cut out a series of terraced flat spots into the little knoll by the edge of the river. He made a spot for campfires and several ledges above it, for us to lay out our sleeping bags for camping. It kind of resembled giant dirt bleachers, which was fine by us. From that day on, the swimming hole was referred to as Sam's Camp, and as far as I know it still is these thirty plus years later.

We spent an awful lot of our youth camping, swimming and fishing at that wonderful spot. The river was deep enough in places so that you could dive from the bank, or from one of the trees overhanging the water, although this activity was usually for older, braver boys. Down stream was a shallow section for us younger non-swimmers to play. We could also wade across that shallow section to get to the island on the other side.

The island on the other side of the river was a farming community called Kiger Island. I knew a number of ways to get to Kiger Island by foot, since we use to raid the orchards by moonlight occasionally. There was however only one road leading to the island.

I have vivid memories of the flood of "64" that closed off that community from the rest of the outside world. I can still see a few hearty souls in rowboats trying to get out. After the flood waters receded, the debris line was ten to fifteen feet above the same road that I spent so much of my youth walking, riding my bike, and eventually driving cars and farm equipment on, while on my way to and from the numerous farms. Out of the several dozen farms on that island, I can only think of one or two that I didn't work for at one time or another.

About halfway across the Long Tom River, between Sam's Camp and the island, was a tree trunk that stuck out of the water at an angle. Those kids that were tall enough could wade out to it. Those that weren't tall enough, but could swim, would swim out to it. I was not only too short to wade, and couldn't swim, but actually sank like a rock trying.

Fortunately Sam would quite often be there, so onto his shoulders he'd lift me, and out to the tree trunk he'd take me. Once I was out to the trunk, there wasn't much to do but hold on for dear life as the river swept past me. But for some unknown reason, that is where I thought I wanted to be, so theoretically I was having a good time.

This was our main swimming hole for dozen or so years. As I got taller and learned to eventually swim, I no longer needed help getting to the trunk, but it seems like Sam was always nearby if I did need help with anything.

As the years went by, they started pumping irrigation water out of Sam's Camp and consequently there was a section of main line that crossed under the dirt road. Dan and I were down there one day, when Dan spotted a big greydigger, and chased him into the empty section of pipe that was under the road. We each stuck our heads at opposite ends of the pipe, trying to get a better view of the furry critter. We couldn't see anything because naturally our twelve-year-old heads blocked out the sun, but we could clearly hear his little toenails scratching on the pipe.

We could here his toenails scratching on the pipe, and yet there we were with our heads stuck into both ends, squinting in the darkness. If that wasn't a pair to draw to, I don't know what is. If it wasn't for the fact that I had been a part of this misadventure, you couldn't honestly tell me today, that you could find two small boys, with such a limited amount of collective IQ.

Dan instantly came up with a master plan on how to capture the beast in the pipe. I missed part of his description of the plan because I was trying to figure out what one did with a mad greydigger, once one had captured it. Dan had captured a couple of baby fox by hand, around this same time period, and I as I recall, the fox got real angry.

Dan had spotted these baby fox sleeping in the sun, a few yards away from their den. Dan quietly crept up on them and as soon as they startled, Dan would foot race them to the entrance of their den. On two separate occasions, Dan scooped up a baby fox using this maneuver. He brought them home, put collars on them, and had them tied up in the hay shed for awhile. I think he called them Myra and Festus.

Naturally, Myra and Festus didn't like being tethered, so pretty soon they escaped. I remember cornering one of the loose fox in the hay-shed one day. I don't know if you've ever looked into the eyes of an animal that was backed into a corner or not, but I have, and I knew that I never wanted to again.

So anyway, there we are at Sam's Camp, with Dan taking off his shirt and telling me to throw dirtclods into my end of the pipe, so that when the beast comes running out the other end, he could catch it in his shirt. That was fine by me as long as I got the dirt clod duty and not the shirt end of the deal.

I started throwing dirt clods into the pipe while Dan stood at the other end ready to catch the greydigger. Eventually one of my dirt clods struck close enough to the rodent to send him flying out of Dan's end of the pipe.

True to form, Dan caught the greydigger in his shirt. And also true to form, the mad greydigger spun and bit as hard as it could at the nearest part of his enemy, sinking his teeth into Dan's hand. Dan could feel the greydigger's upper and lower teeth meet together in the part of his hand between the knuckles. Dan quickly let go of his grip (you tend to do that when your hand has been bitten all the way through) and the greydigger escaped. I comforted Dan as best I could by saying " *The greydigger probably had rabies, so your not only gonna need thirty nine shots but you will still probably die a slow hideous death as well!* " Brothers have a way of being there for each other when their chips are down.

Dan didn't die from rabies although he does foam at the mouth periodically, but then again so do all of his brothers.

A summer or two earlier Dan and I were camping with two of Sam's brothers who were also our age. Dan and I couldn't have been but about ten and eleven, or eleven and twelve at the most.

When small boys camp alone, their dreams are mostly of being pirates or cowboys and such. Whatever we were dreaming, our dreams were interrupted when Sam and Linda came down at the crack of dawn and fixed us a breakfast over the campfire.

I'm guessing that there might have been bacon and eggs on the menu but I really don't remember. Looking back now however, I'm sure that there must have been. I ate a lot of meals at Sam's house and the one thing I know about farmers, is that they eat well. You can't find bacon like they eat, at any grocery store.

I remember Linda whipping up a big batch of pancake batter, pouring it on a griddle over the fire and suddenly realizing that she had brought everything down to Sam's Camp, except a spatula. Thank goodness she remembered what our folks had always taught us and that was to use what you have, rather then whining about what you didn't have. In a heart beat Linda improvised and flipped the flapjacks with the hatchet we'd been using to cut our firewood with.

They weren't the prettiest pancakes I'd ever seen, but I'd have to honestly say that over the decades, some of the best pancakes I've ever tasted were those whipped up at Sam's Camp so many years ago. Even with the slight pitch aftertaste.

Hey, I'm just kidding about the pitch Sis, put the hatchet back down.

SODA

As a semi-normal boy (?) I loved soda pop as much as the next little kid. Well, I should say I liked most sodas. Well, OK, you got me, I liked orange and grape soda and that was pretty much it. I couldn't stand root beer or any of the cola drinks invented in the last hundred years. Call me a weenie if you like, but as a child my taste buds wanted fruit flavors and had zero tolerance for anything else. I'm old enough now and secure enough in my masculinity to admit to this fruit flavored soda preference.

I tried all the colas, only because in the fifties and sixties, that seemed to be the only soda that anybody drank, which pretty much sucked. I can say it sucked now because I'm forty-two years old and have less fear of parental reprimands. If I had said something sucked back when I was growing up, my growing up would have ceased toot sweet. Back then parents had the legal right to execute their children for saying that something sucked. You could think it, but for God sakes you didn't want to say it.

Anyway, anytime we went to a barbecue, picnic, wedding, funeral, church social, Bar Mitzvah, rodeo, roundup or hanging, there would be a blatant lack of fruit sodas. Well you got me, I'd never been to a church social or Bar Mitzvah before, but the fact remains that there was a shortage of fruit sodas everywhere we did go, and probably also at those places where we didn't go.

Of all the fruit sodas, I preferred Nesbitts orange, with their grape bringing up a close second. If there no Nesbitts, I was stuck with all the other brands. Shasta was a big favorite for a lot of people, but it had too much carbonation for my sensitive little mouth. I couldn't even handle Fizzies during my youth.

It was a rare occasion that we had snack foods or pop at my house while growing up. Traditionally, it was water and a grocery bag full of popcorn while we all gathered to watch *Saturday Night At The Movies* on the television set.

On the rare occasions that we did have store bought snacks and sodas in the house, if I were to eat a bunch of chips and cheese curls and then straight shot an orange Shasta, there would quickly be chunky, orange foam all over the floor. Because of this unexplainable foam reaction, my mom soon taught me to pour the soda into a drinking glass, and then pour it into another glass, over and over again, until I got rid of those pesky bubbles. It was a nuisance, but it did work, and my mom no longer had to worry about the floor during the movie. Because of this maneuver I learned to tolerate more brands of fruit sodas.

Another soda I grew to enjoy was Canada Dry grapefruit. They sold it in the snack shack out in the bean field where I lived for about a decade. Well you got me again, I didn't really live in a bean field, but when you spend a dozen summers, planting, training, and then picking those damn beans, you begin to suspect that you'll start getting your mail there also.

On occasion, Brother Doug would come out to the bean row where Dan I were picking and tell us that he had a special assignment for us. Doug was a bean boy, which meant he got to weigh the beans and also haul the bins full of beans around on a tractor, rather than picking them. Doug would stop by our row whenever he accidentally tipped one of the bins over while stacking them on the truck that would haul them to the cannery.

Doug was under the misconception that he could rent Dan and I, for the price of a soda each, to have us hand scoop the fifteen hundred pounds of beans back into the bin, just so he could finish loading it onto the truck. Well Doug misjudged just how simple Dan and I were. He wasn't dealing with two dumb kid brothers.

Well actually, he was dealing with two dumb kid brothers, but if he thought we were going to hand scoop three quarters of a ton of beans, for a cold soda on a hot day, he was dreaming. Dan and I figured it was gonna cost him a candy bar in addition to the soda. The price of two sodas and two candy bars cost Doug an hours pay every time he dumped a load of beans, so he made damn sure not to dump them too often.

As time went by, I also learned to accept the taste of Fanta sodas of the orange or grape variety. I pretty much had to accept it because three quarters of a mile from our house was a pop machine at the airport, and Fanta was all it offered. You either learned to like it or you could pedal your bike three miles into town for more options. Naturally, I learned to like Fanta.

Many years have passed since those days, and I don't drink much pop anymore. Well actually, I do on occasion but I prefer it in a glass with ice cubes and a little something extra in it for my arthritis.

In the fall of 1996, I flew by myself to Puerto Vallarta, Mexico. About ten miles south of town, I stumbled on a gentleman who rented me one of his horses and he led me deep into the jungle. I rode one of his old nags for seven miles deep into the jungle, wondering the whole time if there wasn't going to be a glue factory at the end of the trail.

Surprisingly the old nag made it and at the end of that nasty trail was a waterfall. Because of centuries of erosion, this waterfall allowed you to slide off of it and into a pool of water. This also happened to be the movie set where

Arnold Schwarzenegger had filmed the movie *Predator.* When I had returned from Mexico, I watched that movie with my boys and pointed out a number of familiar spots.

Someone had converted the set into a primitive at best, open air restaurant, that was built alongside the waterfall. It was very hot and humid when I was there, so I slid off the waterfall a few times to try and cool off. That helped a little, but I still needed to quench my thirst, since the seven-mile jungle trail ride had drained me of both patience and perspiration.

I walked up to the bar, pretty much resigned to having one of the region's renowned, icy Margarita's. When I went to order my drink however, I noticed an old friend behind the bar in the form of an ice cold Fanta orange soda.

Thirty strange years had passed since I last tasted or had even seen, a Fanta orange soda. I have quenched my thirst all over the United States and several other outlying countries, without spotting one of these elixir's of my youth. I realized that the Margarita would have to wait.

When I think of all my travels, I would've guessed that I would've found a Fanta orange soda sooner, than the one I was drinking that day, deep in the Mexican jungle.

OOPS!

There are few non-cursing words that sum up a situation more clearly than *OOPS*! If I reach way back into my mental attic, I am sure that *OOPS* was not only one of my first words spoken, but I still manage to use it on an almost daily basis.

One of my first recollections of the word occurred one day in the late 1950's, when my kid brother Dan had decided to take the wood mallet from a peg pounder toy and go outside to do some serious pounding.

I'm sure you all know the peg pounder I'm speaking of. It's that confounded toy that you pound colored pegs through with a wooden mallet, and then flip the contraption over and pound the pegs back through again. A small child will do this all day long with complete awe. While this is very cute to watch a small child do, it is kind of pathetic to watch the small child's father pounding on that same toy over and over again with the same look of complete awe. This may prove that most males never really grow up, but we already knew that didn't we.

Anyway, with wooden mallet in hand, three-year-old Dan marched outside and went into what can only be described as a *pounding frenzy*. We had all been watching for months as our father had been rebuilding the house we were living in so it was only natural that each of us kids wanted in on some of the action. What was unnatural was Dan choosing the tail-lights of my parents brand new, two tone, goose turd green 1957 VW Bus.

This wasn't an act of violence or anger. I think Dan just wanted to play with the pretty red pieces of glass. As his four-year-old brother, I can attest to the fact that these pieces of glass were very intriguing, especially when looking at the sun. Looking through these taillights gave the whole world a reddish tone, which was very enchanting. Very enchanting that is, until our mom suddenly came into view.

We put the taillight pieces down and I'll be darned if she didn't still have a reddish tone about her. Our mom had glorious red hair and freckles, but at this particular moment she seemed to have a little more color in her cheeks than usual. As our southern cheeks soon discovered, she was impressed neither with the pounding incident nor with Dan's heartfelt "*OOPS!*"

A year or so later found Dan and I watching our older (*and theoretically smarter*) brothers, holding thermometer races in the bathroom. A thermometer race means shaking a thermometer until all the mercury is in the bulb at the bottom. At which point, one of my older brothers (***Jim, as god is my witness, it was Jim***) would jam the thermometer into the open faced wall heater, being critical to get it as close to the exposed red hot coils as possible. All four of us boys would squeeze our little round heads in real close and watch how quickly the mercury would shoot to the top.

It was shortly after that point that my three brothers watched the end of the thermometer blow up and into my eye. There was only one thing for me to do, and that was to roll around on the floor screaming bloody murder. There was only one thing for my brothers to do and that was to run out of the bathroom individually yelling "*OOPS!*" That left only one thing for my parents to do and that was to rush into the bathroom shouting at my departing brothers "*Get out of the way, we'll kill you later!*"

I remember my folks picking me up and hauling me to their bed. One of them held my writhing body down with my eye wide open, while the other poured pitcher after pitcher of water into my eye in hopes of flushing out any broken glass and mercury. Good times indeed.

A handful of years later finds me surprisingly with perfect vision, and trudging through the swamps of some far off jungle. *Small boys find mental adventure on a daily basis. I can't really tell you when they lose this ability since I'm past forty and still finding it fairly regularly.*

So there I was hacking away at vines and killer snakes, armed only with my trusty machete, when suddenly I spotted a killer python between my legs. (*I know what you're thinking and shame on you!*)

With cat like reflexes I swung my machete down and hit my mark. The wounded snake immediately sprayed me in the eyes. Because of this maneuver, I knew that it obviously wasn't a python, but could only be the dreaded ***Spitting Cobra of Africa!*** *The Spitting Cobra of Africa has the ability to spit into it's victims eyes from up to eight feet away, thus blinding and causing the victim great pain. This also makes the victim totally defenseless.*

While it was true that I was momentarily blinded during this encounter, I noticed that I was experiencing no pain, which meant that the serpent had to be something other, then a Spitting Cobra.

My eyes and head cleared as the cold shower of water woke me from my little adventure. I was no longer in a far off swamp but safely back in my own backyard, straddling the ditch out by the round corral. I looked down and realized that during my mind warp, I had planted my machete into the 2" plastic pipe that my dad had buried partially underground to get water out to the pasture. *OOPS!*

A few years later as a teenager with a driver's license, I

could be found pruning Christmas trees for a couple a bucks an hour. A bunch of us were out in the middle of a field of these trees with a gas powered air compressor, which ran our noomatic (*that ain't right*) neumetric (*not even close*) neo???, oh heck, they were air-powered pruning shears.

Anyway, I was working on a hundred-foot row of trees, which meant that I would drag the shears and a hundred foot of airline down each row. I would then prune the trees one at a time back towards the air compressor. When I had finished a row I would push the air compressor to the next row and once again drag my shears and airline to the end of the new row and commence pruning back.

As is most agricultural work, this was both physically demanding and mind-numbing at the same time, although thank god we were using newh.... nuh....neh.... (Air-powered) pruning shears. All we had to do was pull the trigger on these shears and they would make a *chush* sound as they effortlessly cut the limbs. You had to be very careful that your fingers holding the branches didn't get too close however, since the shears didn't care whether they were cutting through wood or bone.

I had just finished pruning a row, pushed the air-compressor forward, and commenced dragging the hose to the end of the next row. What you have to understand is that when you finish pruning a hundred foot row of trees and drag your hose down the next row, your pulling your hose out of the previous row at the same time. This means that the first tree in your new row (the last tree pruned on your way back) is acting as a corner post for the hundred feet of hose to rub against while your dragging it to the end of the new row.

I was on my umpteenth row of these darn trees and

pruning my way back to the first tree of the row, and I'll be honest here, my mind was wandering to better places to be and more fun things to be doing. By the time I had pruned my way back to the corner post tree on that particular row, I was once again in some far off jungle, fighting vines and killer cobras. This time armed only with a pair of nee....noo....neyu....(Air powered) pruning shears.

I reached under the tree, blindly grabbed a limb with my left hand, pulled the trigger with my right and watched as the ground exploded in a cloud of dust. It is quite possible that I shouted to the other tree pruners "***Run for your lives, I've got a Dust Spitting Killer Cobra over here! Don't worry about me, just try to save yourselves!***" That's just the sort of guy I am. Warning people of danger that isn't really there is my middle name.

What had happened was that I had pulled the trigger and caused my nih....noo....ner... (Air-powered) shears to cut through the very air hose powering my shears. While I was engulfed in this cloud of dust it was only natural that the flailing air hose would take on the appearance of a highly agitated Dust Spitting Killer Cobra. *OOPS!*

FIRE

One of my first recollections of fire occurred when I was about three or four years of age. It was the late fifties and my family and I were heading to Tijuana to visit my mom's brother Shorty. Of my mom's dozen brothers and sisters, none of them had height going in their favor and as is evident by his name, Shorty was obviously no exception. Shorty was however an accomplished jockey who was actually in the racing sequence of the movie National Velvet starring Elizabeth Taylor.

Somewhere along that trip, my parents left us five youngsters in the car while they went to register at a motel. Anyway I think it was a motel. It may have been a gas station, police station or fire station for all I know, but I'm leaning towards motel. Although a fire station might have been more comforting as it turned out.

At least some of us youngsters were asleep and I'm guessing I was one of them. As I said, I was only about four years old at the time, which put my brothers Doug and Jim at about age six and seven. As luck would have it, one or both of them found my dad's can of lighter fluid and some matches.

While growing up we would watch our dad fill his Zippo lighter with lighter fluid every night. The best part of this show came when he would intentionally set a flame to his hand to burn off the excess fluid from the filling process. His hand would be on fire and he would just calmly roll it around in the air. This was very intriguing to all of us wide-eyed youngsters. Quite possibly too intriguing.

So there I am asleep in a car somewhere near Tijuana with two older brothers armed with lighter fluid and matches. Well, you know that knot type bone on the inside of your ankle? I woke up to it being on fire. It wasn't a big fire, but it was one heck of an attention getter.

I was too young to tell if this had been an accident, although four decades later I have my suspicions, because let's be realistic here for just a minute. Just how on earth do you accidentally set fire to your younger brother's foot? And just why would you want to? OK, cancel that last question, I just remembered that I also have a younger brother and the answer is quite obvious.

Anyway, as semi-normal males, whenever we found matches we'd light em, and of course whenever our parents caught us, they'd whoop us. You would think that these regular whoopings would have stopped us from playing with matches, but in all actuality it neither stopped nor slowed us down. We just worked a lot harder at not getting caught.

During my youth I was quite a rock hound. I had become a rock hound because I spent a lot of time during swimming season wearing an arm cast. While every one else was swimming, I'd be walking up and down the river with my bucket, collecting rocks. Because of a series of lengthy periods wearing these casts, I wound up with a first class collection of rocks that I kept out by the tool shed.

One evening I wanted to inspect my rocks real bad but couldn't find a working flashlight to save my soul. Suddenly a light bulb went on over my head. It wasn't of a high enough wattage to illuminate my rock collection, but it did represent an idea forming in my ten-year-old mind.

I grabbed a hammer, a Sears Roebuck catalog, a twenty penny nail, and went outside and proceeded to drive that twenty penny nail through the catalog and into the cedar shake wall of the tool shed. The catalog was now impaled about two feet above my rock collection. I then lit the first page on fire. It slowly burned upwards while simultaneously lighting the next page or two. The pages would slow down and pretty much go out as the fire got up towards the spine of the catalog, but by then the next page had lit and so this process went, over and over and over again.

It was a perfect night-light for my rock studying. Oh sure, there were a few drawbacks. Firelight isn't as clear as electric light, and of course the burnt pages of the catalog would occasionally fall on the rock collection I was trying to inspect, but I could just fan these ashen pages away and keep studying the rocks. As I would fan these fallen pages, they would disintegrate, once again exposing my rocks. I faced an occasional moral dilemma when the ashen pages of the lingerie section started falling. Pretty girls or pretty rocks, what to do?

I really can't tell you how long this torch did the slow burn but I'm guessing it was just under an hour. Unbeknownst to me, it did burn long enough to also put a two-foot long scorch mark on the wall of the shed.

I didn't discover that scorch mark until the next day. My first thought was that aliens had landed and blasted the wall for no good reason. My second thought was that regardless of the alien invasion, I was probably in for another whooping.

I knew I had to destroy the evidence before the old man got home, so I scrubbed off all the scorch marks which unfortunately just showed me how deep the damage was. With the black soot now gone, in its place was recessed, virgin wood. All of the scrubbing had removed that old weathered look consistent with the rest of the shed.

I spent the next couple of hours giving that section of

the shed this ten year olds version of speed weathering by rubbing about a bucket of dirt clods over the charred section and then spreading outwards until I felt there was consistent look. It must have worked because I never got a whooping. Anyway no whooping specifically for that crime.

Although for the next month, each time the old man walked by, he'd glance towards that section of wall, pause momentarily, shake his head, and then continue on his way muttering "*I don't know what the hell happened to that wall, or which boy did it, but one of em did something, and as soon as I get done putting in 16 hour days, heads are going to roll.*" Well, neither of my parents ever got done putting in 16-hour days, so consequently my head never rolled. Anyway, not specifically for that crime.

Some months later, I was having a discussion with my kid brother Dan. The discussion was based upon whether or not gas on water would ignite. After much discussion I said "*Enough debate and senseless rhetoric, let us go forth and field test my hypothesis.*"

Well OK, you got me, in all honesty, that probably isn't exactly what I said. What I actually said was more like " *I got an idea! Lets take a bottle of gas down to the slough at the bottom of Radke's hill, dump it in and see if we can light it.*" And that's exactly what we did.

At the base of Radke's hill the gravel road crossed the slough to get to the farm on the other side. During the summer months you could drive down the hill and through the shallow section of slough, and onto the neighboring farm. During the rainy months, the slough would rise and crossing it by vehicle went from uncomfortable to impossible. When the slough eventually dropped, it left some pretty impressive mud puddles however. Mud puddles perfect in my mind for pouring gas onto and then lighting on fire.

I poured the gas into the puddle, struck a match and tossed it in. It not only lit, but the flames were high enough that they started scorching an overhanging tree. My first reaction was to throw water on the tree but unfortunately, the only water around was on fire. I hadn't counted on this. That was the motto of my youth. "*I hadn't counted on this!*"

The last thing I needed was to be involved in a forest fire so I tried to kick dirt on the puddle to smother the inferno. The problem was that it was a gravel road I was standing on so all I could do was kick rocks at the flaming puddle. This effort just caused a lot of splashing of the firewater thus igniting roadside grasses. This was typical of the second motto of my youth. "*I hadn't counted on this either!*"

So there I am stomping out the roadside flames, right beside a mud puddle on fire, with an overhanging tree that is seriously thinking about bursting into flames, when Old Man Radke comes running down the hill shouting "*Just what the Sam Hill is going on here?*"

My first thought was to point out that this was not Sam's Hill, but Radke Hill, and since he was Old Man Radke, he should know this. *There was an awful lot of slow people around when I was growing up and I was just dying to point them out, but I chose not to take that path, choosing instead a more familiar trail amongst ten year old boys when they are caught red-handed, and that is to lie.*

I told him that we had just walked down the hill, discovered a mud puddle on fire, while a group of hooligans were running away, and that maybe we should get a medal for risking our lives trying to put out the fire.

We didn't get any medals but we didn't get a whooping

either, so it was kind of a push. We were a little unsettled over the whole ordeal and seriously contemplated counseling but chose instead to go skinny-dipping down at Sam's camp (no relation to Sam Hill.)

As soon as we hit the water, all fires were out and life was once again on an even keel.

WIND

My first encounter with devastating winds occurred at the tender age of three. I had just wandered outside and onto our cement steps, which were taller than I was. Suddenly a big gust of wind came along blowing me clean off the porch and headlong into the gravel driveway. The resulting mental and physical head wounds were so severe that even today, some forty years later, when I look into the mirror all I see is a balding, old man with extremely limited mental facilities. It is really very sad.

The winds of destruction followed me throughout my childhood, with the most memorable being those of the Columbus Day Storm. This happened while I was in grade school during the fall of 1962.

While the storm was putting the boots to the Oregon coast, news had reached The Willamette Valley that the apocalypse was heading our way toot sweet and that we had better batten down the hatches. Those in charge, closed schools early, loaded us kids on our respective buses and sent us on our merry way.

The highway leading to my house was lined with wooden power poles and the arrival of the winds had already snapped quite a large percentage of these off at ground level. The poles and power lines that hadn't snapped were holding the broken ones semi-upright like drunken marionettes. Each time another gust of wind came along, sections of the power lines and poles would dip down almost touching the highway.

While my bus cautiously went through these sections, I remember our driver timing the dipping of the power poles and attempting to shoot the bus through while the poles were on an upswing. He did pretty good too except for when one gust caused a power pole to change it's mind (*and direction*) and smash into the bus. Other then denting the roof and inadvertently causing some of us to leave a few wet spots on the bus seats, no real damage was done. The bus eventually dropped us off in front of our home and we made it safely inside.

We had lost all power and my mom was already working on cooking dinner on our old Ashley wood stove. The old Ashley was our only heat source in those days and with the power out, it became our only cooking source as well. As usual my mom whipped up some great smelling food on that wood stove, which took her five kid's minds off of their impending doom as we just watched and waited out the storm.

I remember looking out our kitchen window into the backyard and seeing a bird suspended in mid-air. Because of the high winds the bird was flying like crazy but just not getting anywhere. Male instinct told me to go get a BB gun, since this was easy pickings. I chose not to since my strict upbringing had instilled in me several moral guidelines.

We were raised knowing not to hunt deer at the zoo or to sluice ducks on a pond. Hunting deer at the zoo is self-explanatory. Sluicing ducks means shooting them while they're paddling around in the water rather than taking them while they're are in flight. Now granted the bird I was looking at <u>technically was in flight</u>, but due to the high winds he just wasn't reaching his destination. The way I figured, he had enough problems without having to also worry about a small boy's itchy trigger finger.

I left the bird to its business and wandered to the front of the house to watch the storm that was knocking over the Coast Range and terrorizing us as well. I was hesitant about spending too much time outside since I had always heard that flying garbage can lids, or airborne sheets of metal roofing, would cut you in half if you happened to be in their path. Since I hadn't seen my eighth birthday yet, (and really wanted to), I chose not to be in their path and stayed inside.

A quarter mile from our house was a cinder block building near the railroad tracks. It was used as an indoor firing range. I watched one gust of wind lift the roof up about two feet and then settle right back down on the cinder blocks. I wondered if anyone was inside shooting at the time. Besides the suspended bird, this was the darndest thing I'd ever seen during my early years.

Just past that building, on the other side of the railroad tracks, was a sawmill with a wigwam burner. One big gust blew the wigwam clean over. This was kind of a good news-bad news deal. It was bad news for the owner that it blew over, but good news that none of us boys had been inside of, or climbing on top of the wigwam at the time, since we frequently did both. The storm was the worst this state had seen, but we survived it with little damage.

A quarter of a century after the Columbus Day Storm I could be found raising my own family in the Sierra Nevada Mountains in Northern California. We were living in a small cabin surrounded by hundred foot tall pine trees. One of these giants grew up through the deck three feet away from our back door, while two others flanked each side of our cabin by no more than a foot. Over the years I had to notch away part of the roof and likewise the deck since the trees had gotten too big for their britches and were starting to do structural damage. Naturally it took a big wind for me to discover this problem.

While the storm was making these giant trees sway, my wife and I could hear the deck creaking something terrible. I ventured outside and could see that each time the tree swayed it was pushing against the deck surrounding it and actively trying to remove the deck from the cabin. The same deck I was standing on. This was not a good situation since without the deck it was a seven-foot drop out my back door.

I fetched my chainsaw and as the tree would sway in one direction I would trim the deck on the backside. As the tree would return I would trim the deck on the front side. I had to pull the blade out, each time the tree leaned or it would pinch the saw against the deck. This impromptu surgery took the pressure off of the deck for the moment but there was still the roof to contend with. Since it would also require the use of a ladder, I decided to wait for a calmer day to tackle the roof.

I remember a windstorm leaning the side tree against the roof so hard that the cabin started creaking and popping to beat hell. We would listen nervously to each big gust and then the snap, crackle, pop of the cabin. We were positive that one of the giant trees was going to crash through our roof. Our thoughts weren't unfounded since during our regular tours of the community we had witnessed this happening fairly frequently. One house had three different trees crash onto it during a previous storm.

A few times the tree leaned against our cabin hard enough to make our pictures swing on the wall. We thought this to be very unsettling until an even bigger gust pushed the tree against the cabin so hard that the front door popped open on it's own accord. This drew major expletives from both of us.

I was watching a different storm one-day with my three-year-old son. The spectacular view out our back window was pine and cedar forests as far as the eye could see. The winds were once again whipping these giant trees around like field grass when all of a sudden I heard an explosion and one second later watched a pine tree crash through our back deck, not ten feet from where I was standing with my young son.

The cabin was still shaking as I picked Jesse up and threw him into the living room away from the crashing tree. Once I realized that only one tree had fallen and the worst was momentarily over, my wife kept an eye on Jesse while I went outside to inspect the damage.

What I discovered was that the top fifty-foot section of a hundred plus foot pine had snapped and crashed through our deck. The butt end of this fifty-foot section missed Jesse and I by ten feet while the top part of the tree punched a hole into the ground almost three feet deep.

Realizing there was nothing I could do until after the storm, I went back inside. My wife told me that after I had thrown Jesse, he became very upset and started crying. He wasn't hurt, he just thought I was blaming him for the tree falling. Poor little bugger.

During the half dozen years that we lived in the high country we adjusted to many things. We got comfortable with earthquakes, experiencing seven tremors the day we brought Jesse home as a newborn. We learned to love the blizzards, even the ones that would dump four feet of snow in three days. And I came to grips with my archenemies, tarantulas and rattlesnakes, both of which roamed the area.

As much as I hate large furry spiders and snakes that rattle or don't, (and trust me here), **<u>I REALLY HATE SNAKES!</u>** I welcome them with open arms compared to the big winds that I've seen over the years.

Many years after the Columbus Day storm, but just prior to living in the Sierras, my thumb had dropped me off in a dusty corner of Nebraska. At the risk of offending these wonderful people, and I truly met some of the finest people that ever walked the earth in that state, there is little to do in Nebraska except imbibe, watch football (GO BIG RED) and watch tornadoes. And in all honesty I did my share of both. I have to tell you that watching a tornado approaching is the most sobering thing I have ever experienced. It is breathtaking, destructive and invigorating all in one fell swoop.

Surprisingly this was the only time in my life that the big winds didn't scare me. I looked into the eyes of a twister and merely speculated on the outcome and the outcome didn't really matter.

When I was little I was afraid of dying during the Columbus Day storm. Nightmares chased me for years after that episode. When I was weathering storms in the Sierras, I was afraid of my wife and son dying. In Nebraska I was all alone. If death decided to tap me on the left shoulder, (*death always approaches on the left,*) I really didn't have a problem with that. As the twister approached, I remember thinking that if it was my time to go, so be it. At the very least I had a front row seat.

When I think about the tornado, and then about the time I threw Jesse away from the falling tree, I realize that I have overcome some of my fears.

Big winds and death don't mean diddly squat mano-o-mano, or when they're messing with one of my kids.

WIGWAMS, MILLPONDS & PLASTIC SHOES

Wigwam burners are all but gone these days but they used to dot this great state like giant smoking thimbles. I grew up when Oregon was a timber state, and it was a truly glorious time. Every town had numerous sawmills and each mill had at least one wigwam burner. A big conveyor belt hauled mill ends and other debris from the mill, into the top of the wigwam where they would drop onto a fire that was burning or at least smoldering pretty much all of the time.

My dad worked at the sawmill in town, where he started out as pond monkey and then slowly worked his way up to millwright. I can remember him taking us four boys for a walk out on the logs in the millpond one day. My not much older brothers Jim and Doug were big enough to scurry from log to log as they saw fit. Dan and I were small enough however, that our dad would hoist us across any big gaps that would sometimes occur between the floating logs.

I remember being jealous of Jim and Doug being able to jump from log to log of their own free will and naturally I wanted to do the same. At one point during this picnic on the pond, my dad told me to stay put, and said that he would return to get me after he finished jumping to another log while carrying Dan.

Well I figured that I was old enough to jump from log to log on my own, so I chose not to wait. I jumped with all my might, didn't even come close, and naturally plunged into the millpond. My first thought was that I was going to drown in the murky water since I hadn't yet learned to swim. My second thought was that if I didn't drown, my head would be crushed between two logs. Thankfully my dad heard the splash, turned and with one fell swoop of his big hand, grabbed me by the shirt collar and hauled me up onto the log that he was standing on, all the while still shouldering Dan.

I don't know if any of you has ever tasted millpond water, but I have a few times, and it pretty much just stinks. Although writing about it makes me wish I could taste it one more time just so I could thank my dad for saving my little butt so many times over the years. It is all too true that you tend to not fully appreciate things until they are gone.

My brothers and I used to play at the sawmill near our house whenever we had a mind to, and the smoking wigwam was a natural draw. We would sometimes walk up the conveyor belt leading to the top or we would climb up the outside ribs of the wigwam to peek inside, but most of the time we would just enter through the big rusty door at it's base.

The inside of the burner was maybe 60 feet in diameter with a big cone of burning ash in the middle. My brothers and I would skirt the inside edge trying to keep our distance from the heat, smoke, and intermittent falling debris from the conveyor belt high above our heads. We also had to manage to do all of this without any mill workers catching sight of us since they generally frowned on this sort of adventure.

Around this same time period my mom outfitted her troop in the latest economical technology of the early 1960's. This was very unusual for her. Traditionally, she always made the most of what ever was available. My mom never wasted much time whining about what she didn't have, she always just made what we needed out of whatever she could find. I'm not just talking about making a silk purse out a sow's ear. This woman had an answer to any problem we threw at her, and there were six of us throwing things at her on a daily basis.

To this very day, if I was to ask her to build me a rocket ship to the moon, she'd not only find a way to do it, but I'd bet my life that she could do it with little more than a few gunny sacks, some old roofing, and a wheelbarrow full of baking soda and vinegar. I have been described by friends as a most innovative person but in all honesty, I can't hold a candle to my mom.

Anyway, on this one occasion, my mom succumbed to the notion that modern technology was the answer to the problem of her five kids, literally eating their shoes on a regular basis. This new technology was of course the invention of the solid plastic shoe.

The main benefits to the solid plastic shoe were: (1) They were cheap. (2) They were thought to be indestructible. (3) (*And this was the big one*) They were so damn shiny that they never needed polishing. Imagine that! A shoe that never needed polishing!

I don't remember how my brothers felt about those shoes, but I for one hated them. They were unnatural and kids at school made fun of them something terrible. The big problem was that they were not only ugly, but also as close as I could tell, they were indeed indestructible. This meant that we were stuck wearing them until we outgrew them or someone stole them, and lets be honest here for just a minute, who in their right mind was going to steal a pair of solid plastic shoes?

What my mom hadn't figured on however, was that her kids would be hiking around the inside of a wigwam burner that would literally melt the shoes right off of their feet. Hee, Hee, Hee. Chalk one up for us boys.

Although now that I think about it, this accidental shoe melting occurred at the beginning of summer vacation and since I don't really remember getting any replacement shoes until fall, maybe we better chalk one up for my mom instead. Damn, she was good.

HANDS

I was sitting in my kitchen, a short time back, listening to music. I must have stumbled onto a very rare and relaxed snippet of time because I found myself just staring at my hands. Since I am a meatcutter by trade, I was tickled pink that I could still order five beers with one hand, but since there was no waiter in sight, this was a hollow victory at best.

What I had noticed however, was how old my hands had gotten. If you've never found yourself staring at your hands on a Saturday night before, than your obviously how old I used to be a couple of decades ago. Back then I wouldn't be caught dead sitting home alone on a Saturday night, but I can tell you this; be patient, your time is coming.

I don't know how old I am right now because my eyes are still ten, but my hands seem to be from a different time zone. The older I get the less time I spend in front of mirrors so naturally, my hands are my only visual barometer.

I think it's because of being a single parent. When you have as much to do as I do, you don't have much time to waste standing in front of mirrors. Besides, there just isn't much in the mirror that I haven't already seen before.

I used to be a small toehead holding a cat by it's tail. As of late that young toehead has been replaced by an ever-increasing amount of forehead and the cat is nowhere to be found. It is so frightening that recently I sold every mirror I had at a garage sale. I even tried to peddle the broken ones, in hopes that I could reduce my bad luck by a couple of decades. No such luck as it turns out.

When I was a small boy my dad worked at the sawmill. One of the many things I remember about my dad during that time was his smell. He smelled of hard-earned sweat and fresh sawdust. When that mountain of sawdust and sweat would walk through the front door, his smell would mingle with my mom's beans, cornbread, and homemade blackberry jam. I'd give all my possessions to smell that once again.

The other thing I remember was my dad's hands. He had large hands like his father before him, but my dad's hands had taken quite a beating over the years. He worked as pond monkey, diesel mechanic, millwright, carpenter, and broke horses in his spare time. You name it, and my dad's hands did it.

When I was small I knew that women painted their fingernails. I would look at my dad's fingernails and wonder why every other one was darker than the others. He always had two or three solid black fingernails on each hand. Over the years I noticed that they would alternate from finger to finger. For the longest time I thought that when a boy becomes a man his fingernails just turn black for no apparent reason. It took me a lot of years to realize that what I was looking at was smashed fingers in the healing process.

I would have figured this out sooner but I never once heard my dad complain about little aches and pains, which was odd because my dad had to deal with some incredibly large aches and pains for most of his life.

So there I was sitting in the kitchen looking at my own hands. I remembered being 16 and setting my hand on my girlfriend's knee. My callused hands would snag my girlfriends nylons just by touching them. I felt really bad. Not bad enough to stop putting my hand on her knee, but I felt bad none the less

Today my hands often sound like a bowl of Rice Krispies when I open and close them. There is so little feeling left that I burn and cut them on a regular basis without even knowing it. I've had a number of people point out that one of my hands was bleeding long before I had even noticed. It is a little embarrassing but than I remember what my doctor always tells me. "All bleeding eventually stops."

I'll be honest, there are some days when I just don't see the humor in that.

About The Author

Dave Whiteman was born in 1954 in the Willamette Valley of Oregon. He still lives in a small town in that same valley, now raising his own children. Dave is a single parent who originally wrote these stories so that his three sons would know of a special place, with special people, during a magical time, long, long ago. His children are his biggest fans and describe their Dad and his book with their quote "Never judge a book by its Author!"

Dave's parents worked in the sawmills and feed-stores of yesteryear, and through example, taught their kids a very strong work ethic and unique outlook on life. They raised themselves and their five rambunctious, hell bent for leather, and just plain strange children, out in the country. Dave thinks it was the town's idea that his family live out in the country as he believes the town wasn't ready for his renegade siblings or their adventures. After reading these stories, you will tend to agree.<p>

www.ingramcontent.com/pod-product-compliance
Lightning Source LLC
Chambersburg PA
CBHW030425290526
45786CB00001B/140